Like a Promise

Like a Promise

Phyllis C. Gobbell

BROADMAN PRESS
Nashville, Tennessee

Poetry quotations: page 66, from "When the Frost Is on the Punkin,"
James Whitcomb Riley; page 199, from "I'll Tell You How the Sun
Rose," Emily Dickinson, from "The Squirrel," author unknown, from
"Multiplication Is Vexation," Mother Goose Rhyme; page 200, from
"Sea-Fever," John Masefield, from "The Caterpillar," Christina
Rossetti.

4273-19

ISBN: 0-8054-7319-X

Dewey Decimal Classification: F

Subject Headings: DEATH-FICTION / / JOY AND SORROW-FICTION

Library of Congress Catalog Card Number: 83-71490

Printed in the United States of America

Nature's promise makes it so,
Fields of green come after snow,
On the coldest winter's day,
Spring is never far away,
Rain clouds move aside for sun,
Morning comes when night is done,
Right will triumph over wrong,
Silent earth gives forth a song.

—Emily Harper
Mrs. Padgett's Fourth Grade
Conroe Elementary School

1

The school smelled of oiled wood floors.

Conroe Elementary was an old school, the kind that the fire marshal eyed with great concern. Every spring the rumor spread that Conroe would be closed the next year, but August found bows and braids and bright shirts merging once again at the big double doors, entering as a single stream of variegated colors. The building was a two-story brick with windowpanes and fourteen-foot ceilings. The oak floors were dark with oil and shined to a gloss. Other inner-city schools built in the same era as Conroe sat locked and boarded as the children living in their shadows climbed onto buses bound for new, sterile, suburban schools. But Conroe Elementary, at the corner of Holston and Sixth, had one of the best facilities in the whole urban district, well maintained, roomy enough to house children both from the immediate neighborhood and the outlying zones. So the broken windowpanes were replaced over and over (usually on Mondays); the fire marshal made frequent rounds; and the floors got their oil, again and again.

Leah Padgett liked the smell. She raised a window in her classroom and thought how nice it was to have old-fashioned windows that opened, especially in the cool of the early morning. There was a comfortable feeling about Conroe, a sameness that was more homey than home. There was even a sameness about the children from year to year. Leah had not made up her mind about coming back to her position until the first of August. Now as she straightened books in the bookshelf, she thought that perhaps the constancy of Conroe was exactly what she needed.

Mrs. Hartsell's voice came over the intercom. "Mrs. Padgett? Are you there, Mrs. Padgett?" Mrs. Hartsell, the school secretary, was hard of hearing herself. It was a standard joke among the faculty that she tried to communicate without the benefit of the intercom.

"Yes, I'm here," said Leah.

"Mrs. Padgett, Mr. Carlton wonders if you could step down to his office for a minute. He says if you're not too busy."

Leah glanced at the clock in the back of the room. It was the first day of school, and the students would be arriving in twenty minutes. She wondered what Mr. Carlton had to say that was so important.

"Yes, I can come now." Leah gave the room a once-over. It was straight enough, clean enough. Maybe not as stimulating as it ought to be, but fourth graders were old enough to know that school wasn't fun and games. The room would just have to do, as it was.

Mrs. Hartsell was on the phone in the outer office, explaining the free lunch program to someone. "Yes, ma'am. We'll send the application forms home today." Bespectacled Mrs. Hartsell, with wavy, graying hair and a red-checkered shirtwaist dress, was a fixture in the office as appropriate as the radiator behind her. She slipped a pencil behind her ear and motioned Leah into the principal's private office.

Mr. Carlton was also on the phone, and he gestured for Leah to sit down. The principal's office, dread of every student, was no delight for teachers, either, Leah thought, although the idea had never occurred to her before. Her eyes took in the worn gray carpet, the cracking green plaster on the walls, the split in the vinyl of the sofa. The room was unfitting for Mr. Carlton, who never appeared at school without a tie, and rarely without his sports coat, except on the hottest days. Mr. Carlton was white-haired, prematurely, because he was only in his late forties. He was tall and rather thin. He stood very straight and walked with an air of dignity. Even as he sat at his desk, he held his shoulders back, his chin up. Leah tried to imagine how it felt to be a student sitting across from him, separated only by the huge, old mahogany desk that was covered with a thin sheet of glass. She could understand how a child would be in awe of Mr. Carlton's imposing figure, even in this shabby office. Leah felt a little intimidated herself.

A full five minutes passed. Leah squirmed in her chair. A few children were already gathering in the school yard, she noticed. Shrieks and giggles came through the open window, and splashes of color danced by.

"I'm sorry, Mrs. Padgett," Mr. Carlton said at last, hanging up the phone. "That was the superintendent. I wouldn't have taken the call if it had been anyone else."

"I understand," she said.

"I realize that the children are arriving. Maybe this isn't a good time to talk. Maybe it could wait."

Mr. Carlton, who was beginning his third year as principal of Conroe, always seemed calm and patient, with less regard for the clock than for the matter at hand. Sometimes the teachers were annoyed when faculty meetings dragged on, but none disagreed that his easy manner had a positive effect on the children.

Even now he paused and drummed on the arm of his chair with his fingers.

"But I wanted a word with you before all the confusion began," he said. "I've watched you during our in-service days. I've worried about you a little." A reserved smile formed on his lips. Leah had the feeling that he was waiting for her to respond, but she said nothing. He went on to say, "I know that you were undecided about coming back. I hope you're satisfied that you made the right decision."

"I am," she said.

"Good. I wondered." He paused again, looking directly at her, gazing, in fact. Mr. Carlton was not really a handsome man. His hair was striking and his posture added a dash of distinction, but it was his penetrating eyes that made the biggest impression. "I had the feeling that you were distracted—which is understandable. I just wanted to be sure that you're feeling comfortable about being back."

"Yes, I am," she repeated. She fidgeted, wishing she could keep up one end of the conversation, but she couldn't seem to manage more than a couple of syllables at a time.

"Mrs. Padgett, I know what you're going through. I lost a son once, too, you know."

He said it so suddenly that it pricked like a needle. Leah gripped the arms of her chair.

"I mentioned it to you at the funeral home, I think. But at times like that you don't remember what people say. I lost my son in an accident, too. Only Roy was sixteen. He was driving on slick streets. It was a sudden death, such a shock. I know what that does to a parent."

No, please, Leah kept thinking, *don't go on.* Her throat tightened. *I'll be all right if you just don't talk about it.*

"I know that the period of adjustment lasts longer than a few months," he went on. "Of course you never really get *over* it." For a moment he looked away, toward the window, but he seemed to be focusing upon nothing in particular, not even noticing the activity outside. Again it was an opportunity for Leah to speak, but she had no words. Even her thoughts had no shape.

Mr. Carlton looked at her again and said, "I just wanted you to know that if I can be of help in any way, please don't hesitate to come to me. And I guess I wanted to say"—he took a breath and seemed to be choosing his words carefully—"don't expect school to work a miracle for you." His eyes narrowed. Leah could almost see question marks in them: Did she understand what he was saying? She still couldn't answer.

At that point, Mrs. Hartsell rapped on the door and peeked inside. "Excuse me, Mr. Carlton, but the first bus is outside."

He nodded patiently, and thanked her as she closed the door. Then he rose, terminating the conversation. Leah stood, too, aware of the weakness in her knees.

"I could have waited to say all of this," said Mr. Carlton, "but I couldn't help remembering how it was with me on that first day with the students. It's been nine years, and I still remember." His mouth spread into a generous smile now, and his voice took on a businesslike tone. "Thank you for coming in. Good luck, and let me know if I can help you."

"Thank you," Leah said hoarsely, and slipped out. Only when she reached her classroom did she realize how violently her hands were trembling.

The first day of school was a half-day for the students. They were first grouped by grade level in various large areas of the building; then each teacher in turn would call the names of those in her class, and they would follow her to their room. The procedure had not varied in eleven years.

The fourth graders met in the auditorium. Mrs. Roark, who would be retiring after this year ("Thank goodness, just one more time!"), would welcome the students and the few parents who had come. By the time their children reached fourth grade, most parents had stopped accompanying them on the first day of school, but there were always some. Students were bused from as far as eight miles away, and there was much moving in and out of the area. Parents whose experience had been with neighborhood schools hesitated to put their children on the bus for the first time. There was a natural concern among those who knew about the Conroe area only by rumor. *What's an inner-city school like, anyway? Are the teachers any good? Is the neighborhood safe? Will my child fit in?* Mrs. Roark was a sweet, grandmotherly type, but a skilled professional, tactful, reassuring. She was the logical choice to do the welcoming and introduce the other teachers, and she had performed that duty for as long as Leah could remember.

As Leah entered the auditorium, she caught a wave of the

excitement that rippled in the room. Who could fail to respond? It was contagious. She took her place at the edge of the stage with the other fourth-grade teachers. The scene before her—bodies in constant motion, faces glowing with anticipation—made her smile. Teachers had their reputations, and children whose older brothers and sisters had attended Conroe usually came with their minds made up. *This* teacher was strict, and *that* teacher was a lot of fun. Later, this same group would complain about everything from homework to lunches—no nine-year-old is supposed to like school—but on this day, there was not a scowl to be seen among the two hundred scrubbed faces.

At the center of the stage, Mrs. Roark straightened to her full height of four feet, eleven inches, and said, "Good morning, students and parents." The walls shook with a resounding "Good morning!" "We're so glad to see all of your smiling faces. Isn't the first day of school exciting? We're looking forward to a wonderful year. . . . "

Catherine Anderson inched next to Leah and whispered, "How do you feel?"

Leah shrugged and whispered back, "Hopeful."

She could have said, "shaky," too, but no doubt Catherine knew that, being the friend that she was.

Not only did they teach together, but they had spent more than a decade in the same church. Leah and Clay had even helped Catherine and Ben with a college and career class until last spring when so much had changed so suddenly.

But Catherine had not changed, not since the day eleven years ago when Leah arrived at Conroe, fresh out of college. Catherine had sat down beside her at in-service and said, "You're new, aren't you? Well, I've been here five years, and I'm a born mother hen. You're going to need a friend, so maybe we can help each other. I need a friend, too. Everybody here knows me too well." Then her whole face crinkled into the smile which was her trademark.

Leah learned that half of what Catherine had said was true.

She *was* a mother hen. As for the rest, Catherine was probably the only person at school who *didn't* need another friend. Leah had never heard gossip about Catherine, only kind words, and that could scarcely be said of any other faculty member. Catherine was a sounding board, a peacemaker, a lively voice in a boring crowd. When Mrs. Roark asked Catherine to call the names of her students, the children vibrated at the edge of their seats, nudged their friends, their heads bobbing wildly. They knew.

They responded to Leah, too, when it was her turn to read her list. Whether it was vanity or just the need to be accepted, Leah couldn't help reacting silently to the children who beamed when their names were called. It said something about the name she had made for herself at Conroe. She wondered how Miss Heller felt—Miss Heller, who believed in straight rows, silence, and two hours of homework every night—when she read her names, and her students lined up, grumbling.

The group that followed Leah down the hall were a diverse mixture of tall, small, black, white, babyish, and maturing fourth graders. The girls wore everything from playsuits to Sunday dresses; the boys generally wore jeans and knit shirts. Every hairdo was different; there were curls, long braids, springy plaits, Afros, stringy hair, fresh barber shop haircuts. Every year at this time, Leah, who had loved *Moby Dick*, thought of the "motley crew" on the *Pequod*. In some years past, she had even referred to her class as "my motley crew." She wondered if she would be able to muster up that much affection for this group.

In the room she called the roll again—"just so I can get to know who you are." She was good with associating names and faces. By the end of the morning she liked to have each child feeling that he or she was a special person to Mrs. Padgett, and to accomplish that, she must be able to call each by name.

"Danny Blount." *Blonde, dimpled, easygoing.*

"Lisa Cotham." *Freckled, auburn-haired, a nail-biter.*

"Edward Curtis."

No one answered. She called the name again. "Edward Curtis."

A big-eyed, little black boy in the back of the room spoke up. "I saw him this morning at the store."

"You know him then?"

"Yeah. I know him."

Several of the students—mostly the black children—nodded and exchanged knowing glances.

This kid has a reputation.

"Well, let's go on," said Leah. "Emily Harper."

Emily was a beautiful girl with dark, sparkling eyes. She was not large, but her facial expression made her seem much older than the others. Everything from the way she raised her hand to the way she smoothed the pleats of her navy blue sundress told Leah that Emily Harper was a precocious child.

"Teresa Kirk." Teresa was a black child with a dozen or more tiny plaits sprouting from her head, each tied with a red bow. Her face was a grin, and her eyes were wide with expectancy. She reminded Leah of a helium-filled balloon, about to go up.

Jennifer Lewis, Joe Norris, on and on she read until she had called all twenty-six names. She wrote on the board: "Mrs. Padgett." She said, "We're going to have a good year together."

They were all very still, for nine-year-olds. They were watching her, waiting for their teacher to entertain them or instruct them, anxious to stop hearing about the good year before them and to plunge into it with every ounce of their energy. They were ripe for learning, this motley crew that had been assigned to her, and Leah felt their gazes, their expectations, enveloping her until the oxygen seemed to be squeezed out of the air around her. She leaned against her desk and took a series of deep breaths. Emily Harper's eyes were narrowed slightly; she was sizing up the situation. She wasn't frowning, exactly, just thinking hard. Leah couldn't look at her. She tried to meet Danny Blount's eyes. He grinned and shifted in his seat. And suddenly, Leah found herself thinking, *T. J. would have*

14

looked exactly like Danny in three more years.

She looked down at her hands. They were shaking. She couldn't remember being nervous about a new class since the first day of the first year at Conroe. She was an experienced teacher, a professional. All these years, she had met new classes and made them feel at ease. Today she was trembling, and every child in the room was uncomfortable. It was time to get out Mrs. Frump, the frog puppet. Yes, she always brought out Mrs. Frump on the first day, and children loved her. Mrs. Frump was never nervous. She knew how to handle every situation. Yes, Leah knew she should get Mrs. Frump. The puppets were in the closet, just a half dozen steps away. So were the art materials for the project she had planned to have the children do. It was a simple art project. They only needed scissors and black construction paper to make silhouettes of themselves for a bulletin board about "New Friends." That wouldn't take much direction. Art was a good way to get started. Yes, she had to get on with it. The children were edgy; she musn't keep them waiting.

She forced herself to stand. "Danny," she said, "would you help me?"

In three more years, T. J. would have looked like him.

Danny had already popped out of his seat, eager to help, proud that he had been chosen. His enthusiasm didn't diminish, even when Leah said at last, "Will you help me pass out textbooks? We need to get them assigned today."

The children were already gathering up their belongings to leave when Mr. Carlton appeared at the door of the classroom. A small boy with tousled hair and an unwashed face stood stiffly at his side. Mr. Carlton motioned for Leah to come to the door.

"This young man is Edward Curtis," he said. "His father just brought him to school. I know there's not much of the day left, but I thought he could get acquainted with you and perhaps get his textbooks."

"Fine," said Leah. She was surprised that he was a white child, because the black students were the ones who seemed to know him well. She smiled at the boy and said, "Hello, Eddie."

"My name's Edward," he said in a monotone.

Mr. Carlton placed a reprimanding hand on his shoulder and said, "Edward, I expect you to cooperate with Mrs. Padgett, and I know you'll enjoy being in her class." Then to Leah, "Now, if you'll show Edward where to sit, . . . " and he gave the boy a gentle push.

"Of course. Edward," she pointed to the vacant desk, "that's yours. We've been waiting for you. I believe you know some of the boys." Edward swaggered across the room, paying her no attention. The children's expressions ranged from awe to admiration to contempt. In any case, Edward Curtis had made an impression.

Mr. Carlton glanced at Leah, his eyes expressing what he would never dare put into words: *This kid is a trouble-maker.* With his back to the classroom, he said softly, "Come by the office later. I'll fill you in."

The principal had barely left the room, and Leah had hardly had time to reach the stacks of textbooks when an "Ouch!" came from Corey, the child who had seen Edward at the store that morning.

"Edward stomped on my foot!"

Another shouted, "He did, Mrs. Padgett! I saw him!"

And another chimed in, "Me, too!"

Edward showed his teeth at them and snarled, "Babies!"

It was not as if Leah had never dealt with an unruly child. She had known her share. But this one seemed different, right from the start. He was more than rambunctious, more than rude. Edward Curtis was an angry, troubled child, and Leah wondered if she was up for such a challenge this year.

When the students were gone, even though it had been a half-day, Leah felt the weight of all her ten years upon her. And it was more than Edward Curtis, more than her motley crew and their demands. Today, she missed T. J. terribly.

Maybe I was wrong to come back, after all, she told herself.

2

On an impulse, Clay Padgett called home before leaving work.
"Hi. How was the first day of school?" he asked.

"Oh, so-so. Not bad," said Leah. Clay had hoped to hear
something like, "It was wonderful!" But if he was right about
what he *thought* he heard in Leah's voice, at least she was trying
to be positive. That was a step in the right direction.

"Are you tired?" he asked. "I'll spring for a meal out. A
hamburger, or—tell you what—just to celebrate the first day of
school for the schoolmarm, I'll treat you to dinner at Lorenzo's.
Do you feel like Italian?"

A little laugh came across the wires. "It's a nice thought, but
let's do it another time. I really *am* tired tonight."

Another time. Leah's favorite phrase, Clay thought.

"Besides, I've already put a chicken casserole in the oven,"
said Leah. "And do you know what Catherine did? She brought
half of a devil's food cake to school for me—for us. She said
since I'd probably be too tired tonight to fix anything but a
baloney sandwich, she thought you'd appreciate some dessert."

Clay liked hearing the breezy note in her voice. Maybe she
was going to be all right after all.

"Are you planning to be late? Is that why you called?"

"No, I just called because . . ." Why *had* he called? He wasn't
sure. "Because I wanted to take you out to dinner. I thought I'd
catch you before you made any preparations. But that's OK.
We'll do it another time. See you in a while."

He stuck some papers in his attaché case, notes he had been

making for his Calculus 1 course outline. The semester didn't begin until the middle of September, and for now there was nothing pressing him to keep coming to the university, but he hadn't missed a day. Here, his sphere was defined. He was Dr. Padgett, mathematician, professor of calculus, trigonometry, and analytical geometry. He operated along exact lines and planes, within specific limits. He was in control at the blackboard, comfortable punching a calculator or marking off hours on his schedule. There was a certain amount of security in his cramped, beige office, with the smell of recirculated air. It was the *routine* that had kept him going, and he hesitated to abandon his routine, for fear that he might become the way Leah had been.

He still thought of the days after T. J.'s death in March when he had come home to find Leah in her bathrobe, her hair disheveled. Often she would go the whole day without eating. And then the times—the worst ones—that he had found her sitting quietly in the bedroom with the draperies closed, clutching the red jacket.

At first Clay regarded the episodes with concern, but not alarm, perhaps because he was grieving, too, unable to keep food down, losing his train of thought in the middle of lectures. But after several weeks, when his appetite started coming back and sleepless nights became less frequent, Clay began to realize that Leah's mourning had turned into a deep depression. She rarely went out, except to buy groceries. She had no desire to see friends. Once, Clay suggested that she see a psychiatrist. She had insisted that there was no need, that perhaps she needed vitamins, but nothing more. They hadn't talked about a psychiatrist again; they didn't talk about any serious subjects anymore. Clay knew that his suggestion had hurt her feelings, put her on the defensive. But she did decide to go back to teaching, just a few days later. Whether there was any connection, Clay didn't know. He was just relieved that she had a reason to leave the house now. Any step in the right direction, even a small one, was encouraging.

He looked for something else to stuff into his attaché case and came up with a copy of Dostoyevsky's *Crime and Punishment*. He hadn't read it in several years, and lately at night he had plenty of time for reading.

Carmen Kennedy was in her Audi, backing out of a parking slot, when she saw Clay. She pulled back into place and stopped. Clay watched her swing open her car door and walk briskly toward him. Her hair, curly to the point of being wild, was blonde with a hint of red when it caught the sun. She tossed her head, and her hair bounced on her shoulders.

"Hi!" She was cheery, tanned, with a spattering of freckles across her nose. "I was hoping I'd see you. I dropped by your office, but I guess you'd already left."

"I had to go to the book store to give them a list of the texts I'll be using. Say, aren't you supposed to be on vacation?"

"I *am*. I just came over to pick up some props. Remember, the Community Players open with *Oklahoma!* on Friday night. I borrowed some hats from the school. Our little company is pinching pennies right now."

"I'm sure that will change. You're just getting started."

"Oh, I know. I'm not worried." She reached into her purse. "The other reason I came was to present you with these." She held up two tickets.

"For me?"

"For you and your wife. I'd be honored if you'd come to our opening." She flipped her hair. Clay had known Carmen long enough to realize that the gesture was something that came about when she was not quite at ease. That was about the only indication that she was ever nervous. She was a spontaneous, confident woman, rarely serious about anything except teaching dramatic arts and performing in local productions.

Clay took the tickets and said, "I appreciate the invitation. This is the first week of school for Leah so I can't promise that we can come. But if we can't, I'll get these back to you."

Carmen dismissed the idea with her hand. "It's OK. Pass them on to some friends. But I'll be disappointed. Those are second row seats."

"We'll try, really."

"I'll look for you and your wife."

He could not help but watch as she walked away, the soft folds of her skirts swishing with each step.

At dinner Clay took mental stock of the dishes before him. Chicken casserole, spinach salad, candied apples, and rolls, not to mention Catherine's devil's food cake that he knew awaited in the kitchen. "You were right," he said. "This is better than Lorenzo's. And Catherine thought we'd be having baloney sandwiches." He couldn't remember the last time that Leah had gone to this much trouble for dinner.

"I just felt like cooking for some reason," said Leah.

A good sign, Clay thought. They joined hands, bowed their heads, and Clay voiced the words: "Our Heavenly Father, for these and all of our blessings, we are thankful." The urge to reach out for T. J.'s hand had not diminished, not in all the months that had passed since their child was part of the circle. But he wouldn't let himself dwell on that tonight. There were other blessings. He was thankful that his own pain was healing; and Leah's—for the first time, he dared to hope. " . . . Amen." He squeezed Leah's hand. One day perhaps she would squeeze back and echo the "Amen," as she once had. But that would have to come much later.

"Tell me about school," he said.

"Oh, it wasn't much different from every other first day," she told him.

"I suppose all the girls adore you already, and all the boys have a crush on you."

"I don't know about that. I probably didn't make a very good impression." She held up her iced tea glass, preoccupied with the swirling ice cubes.

"Anything special happen?"

Leah shrugged it off. "Oh, it was nothing." And then, "There *is* one little boy who's going to provide a lot of stories for me. I can tell already." She described Edward Curtis's dramatic entrance.

"You've had problem students before," said Clay. "You'll win him over."

"This one's not going to be that easy. I really don't know what's going on with him yet. According to his cumulative folder, he came to Conroe just before school was out last year. He spent about a month in Mrs. Blake's room, which reminds me; I need to have a talk with her. But his records show mostly B's. Those grades don't seem consistent with the behavior I saw today. Mr. Carlton said that Edward's father found him skipping school this morning and literally dragged him there, and then Edward threw a horrible tantrum in the office. Mr. Carlton even suggested that they go back home and make a fresh start in the morning, but the father said no, the boy belonged in school and he wasn't going to get away with laying out. Quite a scene, I gathered."

Clay smiled. He loved to see her caring again.

Leah was just serving the cake when the telephone rang. She answered in the kitchen, and Clay heard her end of the conversation. " . . . Yes, hello. . . . It's all right. We were having dessert. . . . Tonight? I don't think tonight would be a good time. I have some schoolwork to do. . . . "

Clay knew, at that point, that the caller was Reverend Kent. He had called before, many times, wanting to come by. Leah always had some excuse. Tonight Clay felt a stab of disappointment, keener than on the other occasions when Leah had refused to see the pastor. Maybe he had been hoping for too much, too soon.

Leah went on. "Yes, I'm teaching again. We had in-service last week, but today was the first day for the students." And then followed a series of "Uh huhs" and "Mm-m-ms" and "Yeses." Clay suspected that Reverend Kent was telling her how glad he was that she was back at school, asking her if she was doing all right. "Saturday? I can't say for sure. Let me see how the week goes. . . . Yes, that's a good idea. Just check with us later in the week."

While she was talking, Clay could see only her back. But when she hung up the phone and faced him, he was not surprised to see the expression that he knew all too well. The firm jaw, the cold stare; the fighter, backed into a corner. Why couldn't she fight for their marriage, for her life? Why did she have to fight the very ones who wanted to help?

"Reverend Kent again," she said. "I wish he'd stop calling. I really don't want to talk to him. He should've gotten the message by now."

Clay wondered how she would react if she knew that *he* had slipped a note to Reverend Kent, just last Sunday, asking, "Would you please try again to see Leah?"

"I know he means well," she went on. "I just don't like his persistence."

"It might be a good idea, Leah, just to talk to him." He caught her glare and added quickly, "That is, if you're *up* to it."

She said, "It's not a matter of being *up* to it. I don't want sermons or sympathy either, for that matter."

"I'm sure Reverend Kent wouldn't make you uncomfortable," said Clay.

She said, "Perhaps later. Not now. Maybe you could just tell him that for me. It would save all of us some embarrassment." She had been idly picking at her slice of cake with her fork. Finally, she took a bite and made an exaggerated "Mm-m-m. This is delicious. Catherine is a wonderful cook, isn't she?"

Why, Clay wondered later, did he pick that particular moment to bring up the subject of the tickets?

"How would you like to go to a play Friday night?" he asked. "I have two tickets."

Leah looked surprised. "You bought two tickets?"

"No, they were given to me. Remember Carmen Kennedy? She teaches dramatic arts at the university."

"Your old girlfriend? Yes, I know of her."

As far as Clay could tell, she was teasing. He couldn't detect any jealousy in what she said. There was no cause for jealousy, of course. He had told Leah all about Carmen Kennedy before they were married. He and Leah had always been honest and completely trusting of each other, hadn't they?

"She's also one of the founders of a community theater over in Arden," he went on. "They're opening with *Oklahoma!* Friday night, and she gave us tickets. I think it would be a nice evening for us. A good chance to get out. How about it?"

Leah gave a sigh. "Clay, is *everybody* involved in the conspiracy to get me *out*? It's a little embarrassing!"

"I don't know what you mean."

"I mean that a lot of people seem to think that they know what's *good* for me. Mr. Carlton had a little speech for me before school this morning, Catherine had a cake, Reverend Kent thinks I need a heart-to-heart, and now someone I've never met sends me tickets for a play. Or was it your idea?"

"You have it all wrong, Leah," he told her.

"You mean she just gave us tickets for no reason? It was just a friendly gesture?"

"You got it."

Leah's eyelashes fluttered. "All right, I apologize," she said, demurely. "To you, and to Miss Kennedy. Be sure and thank her."

"So, do we go or not?" he asked sharply.

"Do you really want to?" There was a hint of pleading in her question.

"I'd like to, yes."

She drew up her shoulders. "I just don't feel like being

sociable. You understand, don't you, Clay?"

"I'm trying to," he told her. For an instant, they exchanged looks that seemed to bridge a gap. He laid his hand on hers. "It's been five months, Leah."

"Five months, one week, and two days," she said. And then suddenly, "Why is this play so important to you anyway? What's the big deal?"

"It's no big deal," he said. "It's nothing." He took his hand away.

She left quickly, turning only to say, "I've gone back to work, haven't I? You don't have to worry about me. Please, don't worry."

She spent the rest of the evening in her room.

Clay cleared the table and spent the rest of the evening with Dostoyevsky.

3

August slid into September. At first, the only testimony to summer's passing was the shorter days. In the morning, the sun was reluctant to get on with its business, and the afternoon mellowed too quickly into evening.

Then the fresh morning air turned crisp. Children arrived at school in colorful sweaters and jackets which were shed immediately and often forgotten at three o'clock when the temperature had worked its way up to a respectable August reading. Toward the end of the month, September's own distinct personality emerged in the first yellow and orange splotches on hilltops, in balmy days and breezy nights, in the smell of football weather.

To celebrate the autumna equinox on the twenty-third, Leah had her class cut out construction paper leaves in fall colors and complete the phrase, "Autumn is. . . . " Teresa wrote, "Autumn is a lot of beautiful and bright colors." Corey penned, "Autumn is between summer and winter." Several leaves, including Danny's, expressed the sentiment, "Autumn is football." Lisa wrote, "Autumn is time for school." Then she changed "time for school" to "schooltime." Then she erased "time," leaving "Autumn is school" and a hole. From Emily came, "Autumn is a feeling, like good-bye." Edward cut out the leaf but refused to put down a thought. He said it was a dumb project.

Edward often was sitting on the school steps when Leah arrived. It became a habit of Leah's to look for him as she drove into the parking lot. She couldn't help sighing whenever she saw him. If he wasn't already on the steps, it gave her some hope that he might be absent that day. She could usually count on him to be absent at least one day out of the week.

One morning when the steps were still wet from rain the night before, and the air was cool and damp, Leah came to school to find Edward standing at the big double doors, shivering.

"Good morning, Edward," she said.

He mumbled something.

"Aren't you early?"

"I guess so." He gave an insolent jerk of his frail shoulders. He was a small boy for his age, skinny in fact. Sometimes undersized boys tried to compensate by being cocky, Leah knew. That might account for part of Edward's behavior, for certainly he liked to shock the other students, and Leah, too. But there was a dark side to Edward for which Leah had no explanation.

"I'm not supposed to let you in the room till eight-fifteen," said Leah. "That's another thirty minutes."

"I don't wanna go in, anyway."

She glanced at the thin arms, hanging from his short-sleeve knit shirt, too skimpy for such a chilly morning. She wondered why Edward's mother let him out with nothing on his arms, and why she let him come to school so early. There were a lot of things Leah wanted to discuss with Edward's mother when conference time came.

"Aren't you cold, Edward?"

"Nah."

I shouldn't leave him out here, thought Leah, *not with bare arms in the damp air.* But she wasn't going to her room anyway.

"All right. See you later."

She had promised herself that this morning she would seek out Mrs. Blake. She had told Mrs. Blake, the first week of school, that she would like to have a talk about Edward. Mrs. Blake had said certainly, any time. School had been in session for more than a month. Leah was embarrassed that she had made no further effort to get back in touch with her.

Mrs. Blake was pouring herself a cup of coffee in the teacher's lounge when Leah approached her. "I've been meaning to ask you about Edward Curtis," she said, "the little boy who came to your room for the last month of school last year."

Mrs. Blake remembered. "You mentioned him to me the first week of school. I thought maybe the situation had taken a turn for the better."

She offered a cup to Leah, who took it and thanked her. "If there has been any change at all," Leah said, "it's been for the worse. I should've tried to see you sooner, but—I don't know—I guess it's taken a month for me to just get myself together." Mrs. Blake offered a sympathetic smile, and Leah quickly added, "Edward is making this a very difficult year."

Mrs. Blake took the cue and said simply, "I know how that can be."

"If you have a few minutes, could we talk?"

"Of course. I'm not sure that I can help, but I'll be glad to tell you what I remember about Edward. I had him for such a short time." She gathered up her belongings, a plastic tray of colorful booklets with a math teacher's edition on top, a bulging satchel, her purse, and coffee. "I was on the way to my room. Do you mind going down there?"

"Not at all. Here, let me take your coffee," Leah offered, since she had no books or papers with her.

Mrs. Blake's third grade room was charming. The bulletin boards were bright and attractive, each contributing some positive idea about the students and school in general. One board was decorated with glittering stars on a sky blue background, and glittering letters spelled out "Our Stars." It was filled with spelling papers marked "100." On another, an octopus held the names of classroom helpers. Smiling cardboard animals hung from the ceiling, designating various learning centers. In a corner, an old bathtub, filled with large cushions, provided a reading center.

Across one wall was a birthday train with a boxcar for each month. White paper was hung across another wall, and a mural was in progress. It had something to do with early settlers, Leah guessed, judging from the number of coonskin caps. An aquarium held a colorful assortment of fish, and the windowsill was filled with green sprouts in cut-off half-pint milk cartons.

One large bulletin board with the caption "Conroe Is Fun" was devoted to photographs. Mrs. Blake explained that the students had taken turns using a camera around the school. They had come up with snapshots from the cafeteria, the playground, the library, and several classrooms. They had caught many of their subjects by surprise. In one picture, Mr. Carlton was wiping his brow with his handkerchief. The PE teacher was yelling, in another picture. There was even a picture of Leah, taken from the door in her classroom. The students were busy at their desks, and Leah was standing at the window.

Mrs. Blake was a neat, middle-aged teacher who dressed in what Leah thought of as church clothes. She had the reputation of being a no-nonsense teacher, but Leah knew just by looking at her classroom that she was not at all like Miss Heller, who practiced the philosophy that learning and fun were contradictory. The students in this room, Leah was sure, had a good time while meeting Mrs. Blake's stiff requirements.

"How did Edward fit in?" asked Leah as the two of them pulled up chairs at a round table.

Mrs. Blake picked up a task card and placed it in a creative writing kit. "Keeping materials straight is a never-ending job," she said, and then, "as well as I can remember, Edward had several friends. Mostly the black boys, though. His family lives in the housing project on Third, and there aren't many whites living there."

"I know. I wondered why only the black children seemed to

know him, until I saw his address. But Edward doesn't seem to have any friends at all this year."

"That's strange. In fact, the whole matter is puzzling to me." Mrs. Blake sipped her coffee thoughtfully. "Of course, I only had Edward a month, and it was at the end of school when we were doing a lot of special activities, so maybe he just put his best foot forward during that time. But, generally, he did his work, and I don't recall any trouble. He just didn't impress me as a child who would cause problems."

Leah shook her head. "*I've* only had him a month, and we've had nothing *but* problems." Edward, she explained, came to school each morning sulking. He never completed homework, and he seldom worked in class. Most of the time he even refused to participate in music, art, or any kind of game. The students were frightened of him. Last week, he had broken one child's crayons and marked in someone else's social studies book. The only time he ever laughed was when he was intimidating the other children. "He's such a sullen, angry child. I get the impression that he's almost always on the verge of an explosion," said Leah. "And when he does explode, he's dangerous. Once he threw a book at someone who told on him for trying to stop up the sink with paper towels in the boys' rest room. Another time he and a child got into a fight, and Edward picked up a chair. I think he actually would've swung it at the other boy if I hadn't intervened. But I can't watch him every minute, and he can have four children crying before I even know there's a problem. That's what scares me."

"I just don't understand," said Mrs. Blake.

"Neither do I," said Leah.

Mrs. Blake knew nothing about Edward's family except that his mother had enrolled him last spring. "I just talked to her for a moment, and all I remember was that she seemed very young; *very* young to have an eight-year-old, like early twenties, twenty-five at the most. Some of these girls start having babies at such an early age. If only they'd grow up a little first." She laughed. "Of course, my daughter is twenty-six, with no intention of marrying and having children, and in my opinion, she's waited long enough."

I was twenty-six when T. J. was born. Leah managed a polite smile. "In a few more years, you'll probably have more grandchildren than you can stand."

"Oh, there would never be too many. Never! But I didn't mean to get off on that subject."

"That's all right." Leah stood and picked up her coffee cup. "Thanks for your help."

Mrs. Blake followed her to the door. "I don't feel that I've helped at all. It's almost as if we're talking about two different boys."

She was right. The Edward that Mrs. Blake had known in the spring bore little resemblance to the terror of Leah's class. Maybe something had happened over the summer. *Or maybe,* Leah couldn't help thinking, *it all has to do with the teacher.*

"I meant to ask you," said Mrs. Blake, as Leah was leaving, "do you ever shop at Palmer's Square?"

Leah made a little laugh. "The truth is, I haven't shopped anywhere lately."

"The next time you do, try my daughter's shop. Just a minute, I'll give you her card." Mrs. Blake went to her purse and brought back a business card. "She's just getting started, but so far the shop is doing very well. Most of her customers are beautiful young women, like yourself."

Leah took the card. "Maggie's Rags, Designer Creations," she read. "Margaret Blake." She looked up and asked, "Is this the daughter you think should provide some grandchildren for you?"

Mrs. Blake laughed. "She's the one. Maggie's my only child. But all of her dreams and ambitions are tied up in her shop, and I'll have to admit, she has a flair for business. She takes that after her father, I guess. He's a banker. Oh, listen to me, rattling on.

Go by her shop sometime. And be sure to tell Maggie who you are."

Leah tucked the card into her purse and said, "Yes, I will."

But Maggie's Rags was soon forgotten as Leah passed the big double doors and got a glimpse of Edward Curtis's face. Her mind quickly turned from the subject of clothes to the problem of simply getting through the day.

As it turned out, the day was one of Edward's better ones—consequently, one of Leah's better ones. Better, meaning no fights, no unpleasant scenes of any kind. The truth was, Edward had slept at his desk for over an hour that morning, and Leah had made no attempt to waken him. The rest of the day he had rolled a little toy car around on his desk, and Leah had ignored him. The other students now ignored him as much as possible, too—because they never could tell what might send him into a rage, for one thing, but mainly because Edward was strictly an antisocial creature; in the children's words, "No fun."

Leah realized that permitting Edward to sleep in class and occupy himself with toy cars was an easy out, a course that, before this year, she would never have permitted herself to take. Every element of professionalism ingrained in Leah resisted the way she was handling, or *not* handling, Edward's situation. Other students were certainly not allowed to sleep or play during classtime. Other students were compelled to do their homework and participate in class activities. Excessive absences by other students were reported and checked out. Edward's case, Leah knew, required measures beyond what she had taken.

But she had talked to Mrs. Blake. That was something. One step at a time was all she could manage, she rationalized. Maybe Edward was coming around, anyway. One day with no clashes had to be a good indication. All around, it had been a rather pleasant day, and that was a positive sign. She had even felt like getting out Mrs. Frump, and the children had laughed, all but

Edward. At least he hadn't said, "That's dumb." If he wanted to bring his toy car tomorrow, she wouldn't say a word.

That afternoon, while her class was in the library, Leah decided to pay a visit to Catherine, whose students were having PE. It would be nice to say "I've had a good day!" to Catherine, who was used to hearing that Edward spit on someone or threw a paintbrush across the room.

Catherine's room had much of the same character as Mrs. Blake's. It was bright, cheerful, and inviting. You could feel Catherine's enthusiasm in the air.

She was working at a bulletin board covered in orange paper, bordered in black. "You're just in time to help," she said when she saw Leah. She held up silhouettes of a ghost and a witch. "I usually try to start with a catchy phrase and create a bulletin board around that, but with these holiday themes, I have trouble finding something to say."

"Don't you ever rest?" asked Leah. "This is supposed to be your break."

"Planning period," Catherine corrected her. "I don't think you ever get a break with fourth graders."

Leah didn't disagree, in theory. But she started to voice the opinion that you might as well take a break when you get tired because a teacher's work is never done, anyway. Of course, Catherine never got tired, so Leah said simply, "You're a dynamo, Catherine."

"I wouldn't be happy sitting still." Catherine handed her a pair of scissors and two large sheets of black construction paper with bats and cats outlined on them. "Do you mind? I want to get finished before the children come back."

Leah took a seat upon the nearest table and cut while Catherine stapled silhouettes to the board. "Next Monday when my students are in the library again, maybe I'll do my October bulletin board," she said. "I can't seem to get any ideas." Saying it, she felt a little dishonest. She hadn't given a moment's thought to a new bulletin board.

"You can borrow my patterns if you want to."

"I have patterns. I just haven't had the time to do anything with them."

"Look, you're helping me, so I'll help you. We could do it in the morning before the students get here. If we wait till your library day again, October will be—let's see—three days old." She stopped long enough to run her fingers haphazardly through her short blonde curls that seemed to spring with her abundant vitality.

"Oh, you don't have to help me. I was just teasing."

"I'll be glad to! With the two of us, it won't take any time. I'll bring these patterns, just in case you can't locate yours."

"All right, if you insist."

Catherine was one of those people who naturally and easily took charge. And you couldn't resent the mother hen in her when she only prodded you to do what was best for yourself. If she tended to run the show, it was always from backstage, never from the limelight. There was nothing boastful or showy about Catherine.

Leah remembered well how she had depended on Catherine's quiet control during the awful days in March, when relatives, neighbors, and church friends had swarmed about her, unable to help. They were well-meaning, Leah knew, but their condolences had landed on her ears like the noise of so many buzzing bees. It was Catherine who made coffee and saw to it that lists were kept of callers, messages, food, things to do. It was Catherine who handled the minor crises for Leah. Which shoes should she wear? Was it cold enough for a coat? Coffee or tea? The least decision was monumental, and Leah waited for Catherine to say, "A cup of strong tea will be good for you. Your burgundy shoes will be comfortable. If you wear your wool suit, you won't have to bother with a coat. I'll pick out a nice blouse for you."

Leah's memories of that time were vague and disjointed, partly because she had been in shock, partly because she had deliberately blocked out as much as she could. What she did remember was Clay never leaving her side, and Catherine, efficiently directing them through the motions.

"You probably ought to get the paper before you leave this afternoon. Sometimes Mrs. Hartsell is slow about unlocking the supply room in the mornings." Catherine stapled up the last bat. "Are you and Clay going to the state fair this week?"

"No, I guess not."

"Ben and I thought we might go Saturday night. Maybe you and Clay could go with us."

"Oh, I don't know, Catherine." Leah kept cutting. "We haven't been going out much."

"It would be good for you. Good for both of you."

Leah still didn't look up, but she felt Catherine's gaze as she said, rather abruptly, "Not this year." Last year was T. J.'s first trip to the state fair. There was no way she could walk out on the midway without seeing him on every ride, in every small blond boy.

"Ben and I don't have to go to the fair. We just talked about having a night out. But we could all take in a movie. It's been a long time since we've been anywhere with you and Clay."

"Thanks, but Clay and I aren't going out much these days." She finished the last cat and handed it to Catherine, meeting her eyes only for an instant. "I'd better get back to my room. Your students will be back soon, and so will mine."

"Think about it, OK? You'd enjoy yourself."

Leah paused at the door. "I almost forgot. The main reason I came was to tell you that Edward has set a record today. He hasn't caused any trouble. Since I'm always grumbling to you, I thought you deserved to hear that I've had a good day." She felt a little silly now. The words didn't ring true.

"The first of many good days," said Catherine. "When you begin to get out and see people, things will start looking up. I'm sure of it."

"I see people all day at school. You worry too much,

Catherine." Leah tried to laugh. "I'll leave you to your work now."

"Say, you never came up with a heading for my bulletin board."

Leah looked at the black and white silhouettes, arranged to leave space for some message like "Have a safe Halloween" or "Be a treater, not a tricker." Leah knew them all. She was sure that Catherine did, too. But that was Catherine's style, trying to make the unproductive teacher feel that she had something worthwhile to contribute. It seemed almost symbolic to Leah: She was as much of a contrast in Catherine's energetic room as were the colorless cutouts against the bright orange paper.

"I don't think I can be much help," said Leah. "The ideas spinning around in my head seem a little heavy for fourth graders. They're heavy for me, too."

Clay was late that evening; not late enough for dinner to get cold, just late enough for Leah to take note, to wonder if this was the beginning of a pattern. It wasn't the first night Clay had been late since classes had started at the university.

When he arrived, he was in high spirits. The dean had asked him to serve on a curriculum committee, he told Leah, kissing her lightly on her cheek. It would be an opportunity to have a part in bringing about some much-needed changes in the department. Without even asking about dinner, Clay opened his briefcase on the sofa and began rustling through some mimeographed sheets.

"Won't it be a lot of extra work?" asked Leah.

"Some, yes."

"Do you think that what you do will really make a difference?"

Clay's attitude toward committees in general was not favorable, Leah knew. Clay was somewhat of a loner, to start with. And he had often said that three people working separately could achieve three times as much as three people working in a committee. Usually one person did all the work anyway. And at the university, the findings of committees were printed, bound, and stuffed away in a file cabinet. Leah remembered well that those had been reasons given by Clay, only two years ago, for refusing to serve on a self-study committee.

Clay stopped shuffling pages and said, "I think this is worthwhile. I wouldn't be involved in it otherwise."

"You seem very happy about it, so I'm happy for you," said Leah, trying to make up for sticking a pin into his bubble.

"I'm pleased. It's good to know that Dean Furber has confidence in me. And the four other people on the committee are very capable. I have high hopes for the outcome."

Clay looked scholarly and thoughtful for a moment. Then he blinked and turned back to the pages in his hand. Leah watched him as he read silently, totally absorbed in the contents of the pages. Clay knew how to concentrate, to focus on a single matter and shut out everything else.

"Dinner is waiting," Leah said, after a moment.

Clay looked startled, as if he'd forgotten that she was standing there, as if he'd lost track of time. "I'm sorry," he said. "I guess I got carried away over the potential here."

"I'm glad you're excited about it," said Leah, remembering that not so long ago she, too, had been an enthusiastic teacher.

At dinner, Clay made a too-obvious effort to talk about anything but the curriculum committee. "How was school?" he asked. "Is Edward doing any better? Did you have a good day?"

But Leah couldn't seem to remember anything worth mentioning.

4

People often asked Clay why he didn't try to get a position in Nashville. He always laughed and said that Nashville wouldn't have him. The fact was, he had never applied at any of the dozen or more colleges and universities in Nashville, nor had he seriously considered applying. He liked Arden. He liked the size of Andrew Jackson State University. It was large enough to offer something for everyone, to attract a variety of personalities and ideas. And yet the campus, a pleasing blend of the old and new, presented a friendly, sort of homey atmosphere. Clay was happy with his position, and now, for the first time, he felt that he could have significant input in the direction his department would be taking in the next decade.

Over the years it had been a small inconvenience to drive from Nashville to Arden and back again each day, but not so much as people imagined. Since he lived on the southwest edge of the city, the distance was actually only twenty-six miles each way, and he avoided the traffic that was routine for those who worked in the heart of Nashville. It was an easy, pleasant drive, a buffer between home and work, work and home.

Since T. J.'s death, Clay had actually come to look forward to his driving time. Sometimes his mind served him like a cluttered attic, and he needed the thirty minutes each way to sort out and discard, or perhaps just rearrange the jumble so that it made sense. Sometimes he prayed, not voicing words, but reaching with his spirit to the Power beyond his own. At other times, he tried not to concentrate on anything in particular. He observed the countryside and listened to soothing music on an FM station. If he found himself dwelling on any thought too long, he started singing along with the radio. It was better if he didn't know the song because then anticipating the words became the focus of his attention.

He had relaxed too well on a few occasions, and he hadn't noticed the accelerating speedometer until he was passing every vehicle on the road. Twice in the last three months, he had been given speeding tickets for driving at seventy and seventy-two.

He had told Leah about the first ticket, never considering that she would read into it a connection to T. J.'s accident. She didn't accuse him with words, but Clay watched the color drain from her face and felt the silence reproaching him: T. J. was killed by a car, wasn't he? If the driver had been paying attention, he could have avoided the bike. T. J. might have lived if the driver had been careful.

Clay had wanted to shake her until she believed the truth. The driver was not at fault. He wasn't speeding. T. J. had been riding too fast on the downhill slope and had lost control of the bike. But even so, given all the same circumstances, in ninety-nine times out of a hundred, T. J. would have lived. That was what the policeman had said. Clay wanted to shout into Leah's deaf ears: "It was a freak accident. No one is to blame." But she was in no condition to hear it.

He hadn't told Leah about the second speeding ticket.

Now, since that ticket, he did make an effort to watch his speed. It was not in his character to disregard rules or laws. He found that he could release his mind of other duties and still keep his eyes on the speedometer.

Clay was already in the Arden city limits, already letting up on the accelerator, when a tangle of strawberry blonde hair made him suddenly brake and pull to the side of the road. Carmen Kennedy, checking out the right front tire of her Audi, was seething.

"Two flats in one week!" she shouted as Clay opened his car door. "I don't deserve this!"

Clay came around the car and saw the rim of the wheel resting on the ground. "I'd say you have a problem."

"You're very observant, Dr. Padgett!"

Clay grinned. The rage in Carmen's green eyes matched her frenzied hair.

"I didn't do it," said Clay, holding his hands in the air.

Carmen had to grin, too. "You just happened to be the first on the scene. I've already kicked the tire. At least you missed that."

Clay started to take off his jacket. "Now that you've stopped yelling at me, I'll change your tire. Where's the spare?"

Carmen looked sheepish. "That *is* the spare. Remember, I said two flats in one week? The other tire was ruined, and I was waiting till payday to buy another one."

"People do accept credit," said Clay.

"I don't like to owe anybody."

"It's not a smart move to drive without a spare, Carmen."

She said, "I've made a lot of moves that weren't too smart."

Clay got the jack and took off the flat tire. The only option was to leave the car and take the tire to a service station. Clay explained, "I don't particularly like leaving your car jacked up, but it ought to be all right. There's quite a bit of traffic out here, so no one could bother it without being seen."

Carmen nodded approval. "If you hadn't come along, I'd probably still be kicking the tire and yelling. I never was very good in the face of disaster."

There was a service station a half mile down the road, and when Clay explained the situation, the attendant offered to send someone for the Audi as soon as the tire was ready. Carmen wouldn't have to get the car until that afternoon.

"I can get a ride over here after my last class," she said to Clay as they pulled away from the station. "You've done enough."

"I'm glad it turned out to be something less than a disaster."

"Only because of your composure and your analytical mind, Dr. Padgett."

Clay chose the route to the university that took them past the town square. It was nearer than using the bypass, but there were more stops. Clay wasn't in a hurry. He had left home so early that even with the delays he knew they would make eight o'clock classes.

Nothing about the sleepy square hinted that Arden was the home of a flourishing, bustling university. The only movement in the courthouse yard was from the yellow leaves as they let go of their branches and floated into colorful bunches on the ground. The old brick courthouse with its clock tower was a reminder of the small town that Arden had once been. One store owner, opening for business, waved at Carmen and Clay as they stopped at a light. Another man tipped his hat as he climbed out of his pickup truck. Then he went into a cafe that advertised "home-style cooking." A deep golden haze hung over the square.

"You should never drive without a spare," said Clay, as they turned into a leafy street, passing large old homes with porch swings and wrought-iron fences.

"I explained about that," said Carmen. "I didn't have the money to buy a tire, and I've made it a policy to pay as I go."

"That's a good policy, in general, but don't you make car payments?"

"No. My car represents my total savings from three years of stardom in L. A." She tilted her head, and her laugh was warm and lyrical. "Actually, the money I saved came mostly from my part-time job selling cosmetics. The only starring role I ever had was in a toothpaste commercial. No one was too interested in my acting ability, only in my teeth. I guess Uncle Arthur was right. He's the orthodontist in the family. My father thought braces were too expensive, but Uncle Arthur said they would pay off. My straight teeth did earn me two hundred dollars." She showed off her toothpaste smile.

Clay grinned. Carmen was the most spontaneous person he had ever known. He couldn't keep from being entertained.

"Finally, last summer," she went on, "I got disgusted with the West Coast, and I had saved enough money to buy a car, so I decided to come back home. I called the dean in Johnson City, to see what the situation was there. Of course, my old position was filled, just as I had expected. But the dean happened to know that there was a vacant position here at Jackson State, so I called, wrote letters, hightailed it back to Tennessee, and applied in person, and, zap! I got the job." She gave a playful scowl. "But you didn't ask to hear all of that, did you?"

"I think we were talking about buying tires, but go ahead, please."

"Buying tires, yes, paying cash. You should be interested in this. I shared a room in L. A. with another aspiring actress named Stella Ambrose. Now I thought that was a strong name, but Stella didn't like it. So, for the stage, Stella Ambrose became Amber Starr. I'm not joking. If you had seen any of the roles she played, you'd probably think the name was very appropriate. Anyway, she had no sense about money, but somehow she had managed to get credit cards. She had a purse full. She started using one, and when the payment came due, she borrowed on another one to pay on the first. She played that game as long as she could and then she began making small monthly payments. Of course, the finance charges were horrible, but that didn't matter to Stella, as long as she only had to pay a little each month. Finally, she reached her credit limit everywhere except at one discount store. She held up that credit card one morning and said, 'I'd better use this one before they find out what a lousy risk I am.' So she rushed out and stocked up on shampoo, soap, hose, anything she could find at the discount store that was her regular brand. We counted when she unloaded her shopping bags, and she had fifty-seven separate items. But she used up her limit."

They were on campus. Clay was driving very slowly, laughing. As he turned into the street that led to the dramatic arts building, he thought how marvelous it felt just to laugh, and wondered how long it had been.

Carmen went on with her monologue. "Poor Stella. It all came crashing down on her. She had been trying out for some good roles, but she had to give up her career just to hide from collectors. I moved out, because she wasn't paying her share of the rent, and the last I heard, she had skipped town owing everybody. I couldn't look at a credit card now without thinking of Stella. So I pay as I go."

"Carmen, your logic is so bad that no one can argue with you," said Clay. He pulled up in front of the dramatic arts building.

Carmen opened her door and swung her legs onto the ground. "Thanks again for your help."

"My pleasure. I enjoyed hearing about Stella."

She glanced back and gave her hair a toss. "It was nice to see you smile."

She disappeared quickly through the front doors, and Clay drove away, wishing the trip from the service station had been longer.

Clay had not seen much of Carmen since she had been at Jackson State. He remembered how surprised he had been when she appeared at a faculty reception at the beginning of last year. They had laughed at the coincidence—after so many years, finding themselves teaching at the same university. He asked, of course, where she had been and what she had been doing. She told him about teaching in Johnson City and working in summer stock, and about trying her luck on the West Coast. When it was his turn, Clay tried to be brief. He had never liked talking about himself. He said, "I received my doctorate, got married, and took my position here, all in the same year." Then he added, perhaps a little too proudly, "The biggest change in my life since that time was becoming a father. I have a five-year-old-son."

Carmen seemed to shrink back a little, but she smiled warmly and said, "Well! You have quite a bit to show for—what is it, twelve years? You must be very happy."

"Yes," he said, and then quickly, "tell me about your position here." Carmen was most comfortable when she was center stage. She talked easily about her work. When Clay introduced her to other faculty members, she was relaxed and cheerful. But from that first meeting, there was a strain between them that Clay didn't understand. They were adults, and adults should be able to put the past in perspective. They could surely be friends. Their college romance was no more than a chapter, contained in the space of a few months. It shouldn't affect present relationships.

Carmen, however, had seemed uneasy whenever they happened to meet on campus. She was pleasant, but distant. Clay wondered about it at first, and the only reasonable explanation he could find was that Carmen found it awkward accepting him as a husband and father. He as much as shrugged it off. She seemed to be doing fine in her own circle of friends. He was certainly very happy. There was little common ground between them now. It was just as well that they rarely saw each other.

This morning it had been different. Carmen's chatter and her easy laugh had been so familiar that it was a little unsettling. He had been reminded, for some reason, of the first time he had taken her skiing in Gatlinburg. She kept falling, and each time she grew more furious—she was used to accomplishing anything she tried—and all Clay could do was laugh at her.

They were both in school at the university then, and it seemed to Clay, as he remembered that chapter, that he laughed a great deal during those months. It was not unusual for Carmen, on a Saturday morning, to say, "Let's drive up to the mountains and climb the Chimney Tops." And Clay, who was used to planning, down to the nth degree, would fill up his Volkswagen with twenty-five-cent gas, and off they would go.

That winter, Knoxville seemed to get only rain and sleet, so the snows in the mountains attracted unusually large swarms of students. Not just the hard-nosed skiers, who gravitated to the slopes, but students like Clay and Carmen. They couldn't afford to ski regularly, but the scenery was free. They spent hours in quaint shops that were too expensive for anything but browsing. They ate hamburgers that they could barely afford in dark, cozy restaurants with fireplaces. When night settled over the town, they drove up to the ski chalet and watched the skiers on the lighted slopes.

One evening, Clay was in a hurry to get back to school. He had a crucial exam on Monday, and his grades that quarter had slipped. When they came out of the restaurant—it was pizza that night—Clay said, "We'd better head for Knoxville."

"Oh, please, let's go up to the ski chalet," Carmen pleaded. "It's a shame to come all this way and not see the slopes."

"I should get back and study," said Clay. "I told you, this exam is important."

"*Every* exam is important to you. If you do happen to come out with only a 3.5 this quarter, is that really so terrible?"

When Carmen pouted, all Clay knew to do was to laugh. In a moment, they both were laughing. They climbed into the Volkswagen and wound up the mountain.

The air was cold and still. Carmen pulled her white toboggan down over her ears, and wispy curls framed her face. Clay thought how lovely she was, standing under the stars and the silver moon. He thought he should tell her that he loved her.

"Now, aren't you glad we came?" she teased.

"You know I am."

"You take school too seriously," she said.

Something in her tone grated on Clay's pride. "I thought you knew by now," he said. "I take *everything* seriously."

They started walking. The snow was packed and a little slippery. Clay took her hand.

"Well, I don't," said Carmen. "Life's too short. I'm going to have fun."

Suddenly she slipped, pulling Clay with her, and they both fell in the snow. Carmen went into a fit of laughter, but Clay had twisted his ankle, and he frowned when he tried to put weight on it. Carmen finally noticed that he was rubbing his ankle, moving it around slowly. "Are you hurt?" she asked, still holding her middle from laughing.

"Just turned my ankle. I think it's all right."

Carmen got to her feet and helped Clay to stand. They brushed off the snow.

"If you had been a little more careful," said Clay, "that wouldn't have happened."

"Don't scold me," said Carmen, with a little pout in her voice. "It's not a crime to fall in the snow."

"It wasn't much fun for me."

Carmen was the one to suggest that they leave. "You probably shouldn't be walking much. I'll even drive back. You can just pull off your shoe and rest your foot."

"No. You're a terrible driver."

Carmen locked her arm in his as they walked back to the car. "I'm really sorry about your ankle. Don't be angry at me."

"I'm not angry."

It was the first time he had considered that their different attitudes could really matter.

During the morning at idle moments, Clay found his mind turned back to that chapter which he had hardly thought of in years. It bothered him that the memories kept popping up without his calling for them. It was more disturbing that he found pleasure in remembering.

After his last class, he plopped a stack of test papers on his desk. He had work to do. He was a sensible man—and a husband with responsibilities. All that Carmen Kennedy could be to him was a memory, and reminiscing was a pointless exercise for people not as busy as he. He simply wouldn't think about her.

George Kirby rapped his knuckles against Clay's office door.

Clay kept the door ajar so that students would know he was available and they were welcome. He looked up from the test paper he was grading and said, "Come in," to the lanky young man in the doorway. He was glad for the break.

"Do you have a minute, Dr. Padgett?"

"Sure, George. Have a seat."

George's eyes, from behind his wire-rimmed glasses, registered surprise. "You remember my name."

"You've been in my calculus class for a month now. Don't you think I ought to remember your name?"

George drew up a chair in front of Clay's desk. "Some of the instructors go for a whole quarter without matching names and faces."

"Maybe you don't make as big an impression in every class as you do in calculus," said Clay, though he wondered how any teacher could fail to take note of the headful of wiry auburn hair. George Kirby, who was only a freshman, was one of the brightest math students in any of Clay's classes. It was a great satisfaction for a teacher to watch an ardent student like George soaking up every element of an intricate problem as if it were sweet music.

"Calculus is definitely my best subject. I'm on a scholarship, you know."

"I didn't know, but I'm not surprised."

"Unfortunately," George made a nervous laugh, "my scholarship has to be renewed each quarter, which means if my grades drop, I lose it."

"That's not going to be a problem, is it?"

"If Dr. Lloyd has her way about it, yes."

Clay was not acquainted with Dr. Lloyd except by reputation. She was known to flunk half of her English composition class, stating without reservation, "This is weeding ground." It offended her that students were accepted at an institution of higher learning without having mastered the mechanics of English grammar as surely as they had mastered their ABC's. One comma splice in the first paragraph of a composition, and the paper was marked *F* and laid aside without further consideration.

"I understand she's very demanding," said Clay.

"She doesn't like me." George twisted in his chair. "She writes all over my compositions, criticisms like 'ambiguous' and 'needless repetition.' The truth is, she doesn't like what I *say*."

Clay suppressed a smile. "Just what is it that you say?"

"I say what I think. She likes flowery, sentimental themes, the rose-colored glasses effect. That's not what I write, because I don't see life that way."

Clay leaned back, nodding, wondering if George actually expected him to bad-mouth a fellow teacher. "So you're having trouble in her class," he said. "You don't think maybe the rough spots will smooth out after a few more weeks? You've only been in school a month."

George scooted forward in his chair and gripped the edge of Clay's desk with long, bony fingers. "It's my scholarship. I can't wait for the rough spots to smooth out. I've got to pull up my English grades to save my overall average, or I'll lose my scholarship. And I can't afford school without it."

It seemed to Clay that George was too anxious, that he was doing too much worrying prematurely. But he remembered how the charge, "You take school too seriously," had sounded. "Is there anything I can do to help?" he asked.

George shifted a little more, resting his elbows on the arms of the chair. "Maybe you can give me some advice," he said. He had already been to his adviser, asking about changing sections of English. He was sure that if he could get out of Dr. Lloyd's class, he could do well in English composition. But his adviser wouldn't approve a class change. It was too late in the quarter. Also, his adviser had made it plain that students weren't allowed to change classes just because one instructor was hard. "I tried to explain that it has nothing to do with the commas. It's a personality clash," said George. His adviser hadn't been convinced. "I wondered if you knew of some other channels I could go through to get out of that class. Maybe I could just drop the course and pick up another math course. Could I take English later? I need someone on my side."

Clay said, "I'm on your side, George, but I have to agree with your adviser. It's too late in the quarter for such changes."

George looked at first disappointed, and then embarrassed. "I shouldn't have bothered you," he said, and started to get up.

Clay gestured for him to stay. "Listen, George, I don't think you have to give up yet. It's early in the quarter. You can still pull up your English grades. Have a talk with Dr. Lloyd. I'm sure she's a reasonable person."

"On my last composition," said George, "she wrote, 'Illogical construction.' *Illogical*, she said. I may not be a grammarian, but she can't accuse me of being illogical."

Clay remembered enough about English composition to know Dr. Lloyd's comments had to do with the compositions' literary devices, not their philosophic content. But he could see no benefit in trying to convince George at this point. He said, "Talk with her. Ask her what you can do to bring up your grades. Teachers appreciate that." With a grin, he added, "If it's any consolation, English was my hardest subject, too."

The strained muscles of George's face seemed to relax a little. "What did you do about it?"

"Studied hard and prayed a lot."

George raised his eyebrows. "Prayed? You, Dr. Padgett?"

"That's right." George's face had a tentative expression, a waiting-to-see if Clay was serious or joking. Clay added, "Does that surprise you?"

"You're an intellectual man," said George. "I've never known many educated people who were religious."

"I don't find that there's a contradiction, myself."

Far from being uncomfortable with the subject, George seemed perfectly willing to air his views. He settled back in his chair for the first time. "I'm not a churchgoer—although I used to be. I got turned off on church. My parents really believe in all that, but it's easy for them. They never question anything. They accept all the religious hooey at face value. I never could."

"There's nothing wrong with questioning," said Clay. "I've done a lot of questioning. Some of the important answers still elude me."

George's tone was somewhat arrogant. "You're an intellectual man. What do you find in religion if you can't explain it?"

"Strength. A sense of direction." Clay had not brought up the subject of T. J.'s death with anyone, but he heard himself saying, "My wife and I lost our little boy in an accident last spring. My religion—my faith—has been a source of comfort to me."

George said, "It seems to me that if there really was an Almighty Power taking care of you, he wouldn't let something like that happen."

It occurred to Clay that if Leah would ever talk about it, her appraisal of the situation would come very close to George's. "Death is a part of life," he said. "That's simple logic."

When George stood, he seemed to unfold his body parts and then gather himself up. At the door, he turned and said, "My parents always found strength in their religion, too. I never could. Maybe there *is* something to it, but if I ever got interested again, it would have to make *sense* to me. You know what I mean?"

"Absolutely."

For a moment he lingered, saying nothing. Then he thanked Clay for his time and left.

Later in the week, the curriculum committee met for the first time. Rather than appointing a chairman, Dean Furber had asked the committee to elect one among themselves. Clay didn't actively seek the chairmanship, but he showed so much optimism for what the committee could accomplish that he was the unanimous choice.

The other members—three men and one woman—were enthusiastic about being involved, but no one except Clay had given much thought as to how they should proceed. Clay was a natural organizer. "It seems reasonable to me," he said, "that in this first meeting we should decide simply what we're going to do and how we're going to go about doing it." It was agreed that they would meet every two weeks, and that each member would complete specific duties between times. Clay would coordinate all of the assignments and reports. He actually preferred the term "coordinator" to that of "chairman," but, as it seemed a moot point, he didn't mention it. By the end of the meeting, the committee had developed clear-cut goals and a detailed plan of action.

The group complimented Clay, pledged their support, and reiterated their confidence in him. Carson Lewis, a seasoned professor with more hair on his chin than on his head, remarked, "Who would have thought that after the first meeting we could already see light at the end of the tunnel?"

Shirley Nettleton noted that Clay had cut out a demanding role for himself. Clay tried to minimize the importance of his function, but he was not blind to the rigorous task before him. He looked forward to it. He wanted to work, to be productive. He was determined to keep his mind occupied.

Autumn color was at its peak. On Friday morning as Clay waited for the toaster to deliver his two slices, he happened to switch on the radio and hear a deejay announce that rain was predicted for Nashville, but the weather in Gatlinburg was supposed to be magnificent. Clay wondered why he hadn't thought of it before. A trip to the mountains might be exactly what he and Leah needed. By the time he had finished his toast and juice, he heard Leah moving around. The radio in the bedroom was on, another weather forecast blaring. Leah said, as Clay put his arms around her, "It's supposed to rain this weekend."

Clay presented his idea, complete with supporting arguments. It would be a beautiful drive, he told her, and the timing was perfect because soon he might be too involved in the curriculum committee to take a weekend trip. They hadn't been away for much too long a time, and they both needed a change of scenery. He could manage to get home that afternoon by the time she arrived. They could be in Gatlinburg by ten o'clock.

Leah gave him a sweet, almost motherly smile. "It's a nice thought," she said, "but we couldn't get reservations, I'm sure. With UT's home game and the mountains at peak color, it's impossible. Catherine and Ben tried earlier in the week, and there were no vacancies anywhere."

"So we'll go past Gatlinburg," Clay said. "We'll go on to North Carolina if we have to."

Leah gave a meaningless little laugh and closed the bathroom door. It was if she had said, "Silly boy!"

Perhaps because he had been denied a trip to witness autumn's finest display, Clay was suddenly aware of the beauty on campus, the golden maples and blazing oaks, shimmering in the sunlight. At lunch he shuffled through the leaves to the student center and ate alone, his temper clouded by the early morning scene with Leah. What disturbed him was not that she had come up with a sound reason for not going; rather, that she never seriously considered the idea. Lately, there was no talking things over with Leah, not even any arguing. She was unreachable. Clay wondered how long it would be before she would be willing to break out of her self-imposed prison. He wondered how long he could wait.

He had just left the student center when Carmen Kennedy called his name.

In her tweed skirt and pale blue sweater, her hair pulled back from her face, Carmen could have passed for one of the twenty-year-old coeds. Even as she came closer, her face glowed with that remarkable trait of youth that holds open arms to life. The leaves crunched under her feet. Clay was aware of the sound, and of the woody smell that clings to autumn air. It was both lovely and sad. He had the strange sensation that he was on the wrong side of a glass, looking in on a pageant of beauty, youth, and hope that ought to include him.

Life's too short. I'm going to have fun.

"You must have been deep in thought!" Carmen's words came from half way between a smile and a laugh.

"Was I that somber?"

"*Very* somber. Can I help?"

He thought how easy it would be to tell her that his marriage was in trouble, but he resisted. "Not this time," he said.

"I was on my way to lunch."

"I just finished."

A leaf, almost the color of her hair, drifted down and stuck to her sleeve. She took the stem between her thumb and forefinger and twirled it around, examining it with thoughtful eyes. "My father used to say, on days like this, that fall has put on her Sunday clothes." Then she looked up at him. "I'm driving up to Gatlinburg for the weekend. I haven't seen the mountains at peak color in a while."

"It ought to be a wonderful trip," he told her, and thought of his own backyard and rain beating the leaves to the ground.

"I did buy a new tire."

"That's a smart move."

"I'm getting smarter."

He gave some excuse and made a hasty return to the safety of his beige office. He was a sensible man. He retreated to his desk and leaned back in his chair to get his breath before attacking the papers in front of him. He had work to do.

He had told himself that he wouldn't think of her, but when he closed his eyes, she was still there.

5

Leah buttoned up her heavy coat, which was making its first appearance since last winter. The morning was cold and clear, and the leaves that had colored the trees earlier in October now lay on the school yard in brown rings beneath gray limbs. *Halloween weather,* Leah thought, climbing out of the car. Her students were caught up in the anticipation of trick-or-treating, and had been for a week. Leah was glad it would be over after tomorrow night, or by the day after, when all the candy would be brought to school and devoured. Halloween weather. Perfect for spooks. There would be an interlude of warmer days before winter set in, but Leah had dragged out her winter coat for the first frost. Something about frost on the pumpkin flitted around in her mind. *The frost is on the punkin . . . When the frost is on the punkin. . . .* What was the rest? She couldn't remember.

It bothered her when she couldn't remember a line, or a name. Sometimes she would look straight into a student's face, and the name wouldn't come. What did that mean? she wondered. What did it all mean?

She rammed her hands into the pockets of her coat. A scrap of crumpled paper found its way into her right hand, and she pulled out what appeared to be a note to herself. She read, *Get car washed. Gas. Cleaners—Clay's brown suit.* It was a list of errands to run, left over from last winter. She was always writing reminders to herself. That was excusable, not like forgetting a line of poetry that you had committed to memory. *Hose, exchange T.J.'s jacket.*

She remembered now. Clay had picked up a red nylon jacket with an Atlanta Falcons symbol on it. "Just suits T. J.," he had said. And it did, except that it was a size too small, and Leah had gone on a Saturday to exchange it. The next Saturday, T. J. had been wearing his red jacket when the bike had wrecked, when the car had hit him. . . . *Milk, eggs,* Leah read quickly, *straws, Cocoa Puffs.* She wadded the paper, squeezing it until her nails dug into her palm.

Inside the building, as she fumbled for the key to her classroom, the custodian came by, rolling an oversized trash barrel. "G'morning, Mrs. Padgent," he said with a pleasant drawl. He was a fat young man with glazed eyes who, for three years, had persisted in mispronouncing her name. Leah no longer made a point of correcting him. People with blank stares didn't bother with details, and perhaps they were the happy ones, anyway.

Leah gave him a nod and a brisk "Good morning," and dropped the paper wad into his barrel.

She stuck her key back into her purse. She didn't want to go into the room. It was early. She always came early. Clay started bustling around as soon as the first streaks of light crossed the sky, and the noise always woke her. It was just as well to get on with her day. She didn't like to linger in the house after Clay was gone.

It had all been so different when T. J. was there. Getting him up and moving, last-minute lunch money, cartoons blaring in the background. . . .

Leah hurried toward the teachers' lounge, pressing her temples as the pulsing started up again. Sometimes she awoke with a headache, but she had felt fine this morning. If positive thinking had any power, she had tried. *Believe me, Dr. Peale. Believe me, Clay, Catherine, Reverend Kent, I have tried.* Still, something as insignificant as a slip of paper could set her off. Was it a weak spirit or a weak mind? What flaw in her character allowed her to get worked up over something that no one else could possibly understand, not even Clay? Clay was in control. If he was tense, he could make himself relax. He could talk himself out of worry, pain, even grief, thought Leah. It made her sick.

Catherine had the coffee going in the lounge. "I thought that was my job," said Leah, who was usually the first to arrive. "Why are you here so early?"

"I had an errand to run on the way to school," said Catherine, "and it didn't take as long as I expected. Coffee's ready."

The lounge was steamy, and the aroma of coffee was a comfortable smell. Leah wished she could spend her day in the lounge, with the other teachers going in and out, but none staying too long. She laid her purse on a table beside Catherine's belongings—all the paraphernalia befitting a dedicated teacher, including a sweet potato, which, Leah figured, was for growing a vine.

Leah took a few sips of coffee and touched her temples again. "You don't have an aspirin, do you? I think I cleaned out the bottle in my room yesterday."

Catherine gave her a scrutinizing look that Leah pretended not to notice. "I might. Another headache?"

"Probably the same one I took home from school yesterday. I thought it was gone until a few minutes ago."

Catherine found a pillbox in her purse and handed it to Leah. "These are aspirins. I'll get you a glass of water."

"Oh, Catherine, you don't have to mother me."

"Sit down." Catherine made an elaborate gesture of dismissal, and whisked out of the room as Leah sank onto the sofa.

When Catherine returned with the water, she said, "You ought to do something about those headaches."

A glass of water, a word of advice, Leah thought, but then Catherine wasn't the kind who needed an excuse to dish out advice. "Usually aspirins help," said Leah.

"No, I mean something to get at the cause."

"I know the cause—tension." Then she corrected herself, "Edward Curtis."

"Wasn't Edward absent yesterday?"

Leah mumbled "Uh huh," avoiding the implication by quickly adding, "I'm counting on a long talk with his mother at conference time—if she comes."

Notes would be sent home to parents on the day after Halloween, announcements of parent-teacher conferences on the following Thursday and Friday. Leah had some doubts that Edward's mother would show up. That was usually the case with problem students. Either they didn't take the notes home, or the parents didn't care anyway. But she was hoping. She had to hold on to some hope.

Once, after Edward broke Lisa Cotham's crayons, Leah had decided to call his mother. She dialed the number given in the cumulative folder, but the recording came on, saying that the phone had been disconnected. The emergency number in the office was Mr. Curtis's work number, and somehow it didn't seem appropriate to get Edward's father off of security detail at the state prison to say, "Your son broke a little girl's crayons a week ago, and he hasn't brought her a new box." So Leah replaced the crayons herself, and added one more reminder to the long list in the journal she was keeping on Edward.

"Have you ever had any response from your notes?" asked Catherine.

Leah shook her head. "Edward never took them home or never managed to get them back, so I didn't write any more." She added as a kind of wishful afterthought, "Maybe his mother will show up."

"If she doesn't," said Catherine, "you'll just have to get the social worker to contact the parents. Sometimes that's the only way to get in touch with them."

"I guess so." Leah never liked asking Social Services for help. She was used to handling her own students herself. This year she hadn't even asked Mr. Carlton for help except in a few cases that weren't particularly crucial, anyway. *Especially this year,* she didn't want any experts probing into Edward's situation. A close examination might put her on the line, too.

Her head kept pounding. She avoided the urge to touch her temples, because she didn't want to make a big deal of it, but she couldn't help squinting.

Catherine said, "You must have an awful headache. Maybe you should lie down."

"Oh, I couldn't lie down," said Leah. "You know, you're really something. You notice everything."

"Haven't I always told you I was a mother hen?"

"You need a whole brood of your own little chickens, so you won't have to mother your friends."

"You're probably right." Catherine came to sit beside Leah and said, in a more serious tone, "Look, I haven't known whether to say anything or not, but we *are* friends, and maybe this is a good time." She held her palms together and pressed at her knuckles. "Leah, everybody knows how hard these past months have been on you, and people want to help. But you've built a wall, shut us out. You're asking too much of yourself, Leah."

Leah was used to Catherine's advice, but it usually came coated in humor. This little heart-to-heart was out of character for Catherine, and Leah felt her face flush. Why couldn't Catherine just keep things the way they were between them? "I know you mean well," she said, "but please—I don't need this."

"Someone had to say it. Leah, please don't be afraid to ask for help. If not from me, from someone. For your headaches, and Edward, for the slump you're in, and," she added, "for your marriage."

Leah bristled. "What do you think you know about my marriage?"

"I don't know anything. I just have the feeling that you and Clay are having a hard time getting on with your lives."

"Clay and I are fine. Not that it's any of your business. Frankly, I think you're taking friendship a little too far."

"I don't mean to pry, Leah."

"Then don't."

Catherine gathered her belongings and left, her swift movements slicing through the heavy air like a blade. Leah couldn't look her way, but she had the feeling that Catherine paused at the door. Then the stillness gave way to shuffling feet and laughter, and two other teachers entered the lounge. They spoke to Leah, and she spoke to them. She tried to smile and sound cheerful, but she wondered if they couldn't *feel* what had just happened. Something grave weighed in the air, pressed in from every direction. Wasn't that a giveaway?

But the two teachers, and the others who drifted in during the next few minutes, went on chattering and drinking coffee, unconcerned. Leah caught a word now and then about conferences, a sale somewhere, a recipe for pumpkin pie. But for the most part, her senses were dulled to the conversations in the room as well as to the magazine in her lap, whose pages she flipped regularly. Sometime later, she noticed a thinning out of people in the room, and someone said, "It's five past eight." Leah sat still until she was the only one left, and she watched the clock on the wall until 8:12. The school doors would open at 8:15. There was no more putting off the inevitable.

She had just enough time to unlock her room and position herself at the door. When the teachers on bus duty opened the main doors, students began to pour into the halls like rushing waters. Leah could remember when this part of the day was exciting. In less than a minute, quiet, empty halls suddenly became a river of noise and animated bodies. Then, in another minute, tiny streams began to branch off into the various classrooms, and, suddenly, the halls were clear again.

Such observations on school life had always fascinated Leah. She remembered that Clay had once told her, "I'm amazed at how you can take an ordinary day at school and squeeze something extraordinary out of it." Leah thought, *I used to be a good teacher.*

Remembering that, she forced a smile as she greeted each child. Students arrived at school eager and happy, for the most part. Children like Edward who came sulking, without a word for the teacher, were the exception.

"Good morning, Jason." Her voice sounded pleasant enough, to her. She wondered if it sounded artificial to the children.

"Hi." Buddy Jordan lingered in the doorway.

"Good morning, Buddy."

"Mrs. Padgett, when I was getting my social studies, my mama saw the page where Edward marked in my book, and she said she wasn't gonna pay for it. Even if it was a new book, it was Edward's fault, not mine, and I shouldn't have to pay."

"I understand. As long as that's the only damage to the book, you won't be charged for it."

"Mrs. Padgett, did you hear about Edward?" It was Lisa Cotham.

"No, what about him?"

"He got into a fight!" Lisa's voice was thick with exaggerated disapproval. "It was out on the school yard, and Mr. Carlton came out and took him and the other boy to the office. The other boy was a third grader, but he was bigger than Edward." She began to chew on a fingernail.

"But Edward had him down!" Corey put in.

Leah shook her head, but before she could say anything, Danny Blount appeared at the door, saying, "Look at my face, Mrs. Padgett!"

Leah frowned at the swollen eye and scraped cheek, painted with Mercurochrome. "What happened, Danny?"

"I had a wreck on my bike."

Leah felt her hands grow clammy. "Oh, no," she said, and she heard a flutter in her voice that seemed to belong to someone else.

Danny gave an uneasy little laugh. "I'm all right, Mrs. Padgett. It wasn't anything," he said, going quickly to his seat.

He looked so much like T. J.—or like T. J. would have grown to look—that it made Leah weak. Danny could have been killed, too. She had not seen T. J.'s accident, but she had replayed it in her mind so many times that now it came like a memory; the car and bike, both appearing from out of nowhere; the impact, and T. J., hurled through the air. Did he cry out? Did he call for her? What did he think in those last seconds? What did he feel that instant before everything stopped? Why? Why her baby? How could God do that to her?

Leah gripped the door facing. Somewhere in her body, a loud hammering drove out the other sounds around her. Was it her head, or her heart, or both, keeping time like a marching band? *I've got to get hold of myself.* She took a deep breath, and another one. She tried to focus on what the students were doing. Lisa was putting paper in her notebook. Buddy was sharpening a pencil. Corey and Jason were talking and laughing. She could see their mouths moving. She took another breath. Gradually, the sound began to come back.

"He popped him right on the chin!" Corey was saying.

"Mrs. Padgett, are you all right?" It was Emily Harper, with her piercing eyes.

"Yes, Emily, I'm all right."

Emily handed her a sheet of paper. "Here's my article for the school newspaper. Would you check it, please?"

"I'll be glad to."

Leah watched Emily's calm, deliberate preparations for the day. She stacked her books in her desk, got out her pencils, and opened her notebook in front of her. Her black hair was braided this morning. She felt for a braid and brought it around her shoulder, fingering the white ribbon while reading something in her notebook.

Leah remembered herself at nine years old, a bright, inquisitive girl with shining black braids and dancing eyes. In the fourth grade, inspired by an intense, exacting teacher named Miss Eudora Willingham, she had determined to make her mark on the world when she grew up.

Leah admitted Teresa Kirk and, with a glance at the empty hall, closed the door. She had to try harder, and she would. For Clay and Catherine, and for Emily.

The rest of the school day, by comparison to the first hour, was uneventful. While her students were having PE, Leah went to the lounge for a soft drink. Catherine was there, fumbling in her purse, her back to the door. *I can't take another confrontation*, Leah thought, slipping back out. But in the hall, she paused. The scene from that morning still made her ache. Catherine was the best friend she'd ever had. How could either one of them have let those words pass between them?

She's had time to think it over, Leah thought. She imagined herself walking into the lounge, and Catherine rushing up to her with a grin. "Hey, I was just taking the mother hen bit too far," Catherine would probably say. "Can you forgive me?" That was Catherine. She could never be too serious too long.

I'm probably making too much out of the whole thing, anyway, Leah decided, stepping back to the door, opening it halfway. She heard, "Yes, this is Catherine Anderson. I came by the lab this morning, and I was just checking on the test results."

The phone was in an alcove, hidden from the door. Leah turned away, knowing that she hadn't been seen. She made her exit as Catherine said, hoarsely, "I see. Well, thank you, anyway."

Something in her voice told Leah that this just wasn't the right time.

Most afternoons Leah found a reason to stop at the grocery store or the bank or the gas station. But whenever there were no errands to run, whenever she came straight from school, the hour and a half before Clay arrived home seemed interminable. On these days, she moved through a routine of sorts that she had set for herself.

First, she stopped in the kitchen. Sometimes she fixed a carrot or a celery stalk. She had always watched her calories, watched her weight, although lately, it seemed that whatever she ate didn't matter, that she still remained a little too thin. Today a shiny apple caught her eye. She took it from the basket, along with the morning paper that Clay had left on the kitchen table. Munching, she went to her bedroom and switched on the radio. Some call-in show was airing, but it didn't matter, really, just as long as it made a sound. She changed into jeans and shirt and climbed on the bed, arranging the pillows at the headboard so she could sit up against them. Then she began to unfold the newspaper. If she was lucky, she would fall asleep.

The worst part of the afternoons was the quiet. The noise of the radio never quite filled the empty house. Leah remembered how, before T. J. was born, she used to look forward to that time to herself in the afternoon. In those days, she could actually relax, and she didn't need the radio. "After a day with noisy children," she had told Clay, "I want *absolute quiet.*"

After T. J. was born the opportunity to relax was rare. T. J. was an active, demanding baby, and Leah always felt that the two of them deserved some time just to be together after a whole day away from each other. But she remembered thinking, too, *If I could just have one hour of quiet.* . . . Even when T. J. was older, playing with friends, the noises were there; the door banging, rattling silverware in the kitchen, high-pitched voices, T. J.'s in particular, shouting, "Mom, we're out of peanut butter!" The noises; how familiar they had grown.

Leah didn't turn on the television at this time of day. The children's programs were shows that T. J. had watched, and it was just too hard, still. Once, in the summer, she had flipped the television on in the middle of a children's program she had seen before. She remembered, because T. J. had sung a little song from it. The song had been about family members. T. J. had asked, "Why don't I have a brother?" Hearing the song again, Leah had been rocked by a wave of nausea. No, she wouldn't make that mistake again.

Today, the newspaper wasn't able to hold her attention. The print seemed fuzzy, and some words jumped out at her, while others seemed to hide. She might as well be trying to read in Arabic, she decided, for all she comprehended. She tried lying down and closing her eyes, hoping to sleep, but her brain continued its idle racing.

"Stay busy," Clay had told her, back in the summer. Well, she had just spent eight hours working, and how much better off was she? She thought of running the vacuum or gathering up a load of laundry, but she was too tired for chores. She hated days like this, when her body was exhausted but her mind kept going, calling up little pieces of the past that pricked like broken glass. T. J. jumping up and down on his bed, the way his cowlick stood up after he had slept on it, the tail of his red jacket, flapping in the warm wind as he rode off on his bike. . . .

Leah got up quickly and went to the chest of drawers. She knelt down and opened the bottom drawer. Reaching under the sheets and pillowcases, she pulled out the red jacket.

Clay and Leah's mother had put away all of the other clothes and all of T. J.'s toys. The cleaning woman, who had been hired after T. J.'s death, dusted once a week in his room, and Leah never went inside, never even opened the door to look in. "When you're ready," Clay had said, "we'll go through everything." Leah had no idea when that would be.

But the jacket hadn't been with the other clothes. The evening after T. J.'s death, Jeremy Dylan had brought it by. He had found the jacket in the ditch in front of his house, a block from the scene of the accident. Leah remembered Catherine, answering the door, reassuring T. J.'s friend that he had done the right thing by bringing the jacket to them, and then trying to be inconspicuous as she hung it in the hall closet.

At the time it all seemed unreal, like an illusion in slow motion. But the day after the funeral, which was the first opportunity she had, Leah took the jacket from the closet and placed it under the sheets in the chest of drawers.

It was a silly thing to do, she knew. Sillier, even, to take out the jacket and expect to draw comfort from it. It had no magic, no healing powers. She wasn't that far gone. But when she held the jacket close, something peaceful touched her, if only for an instant.

She felt of the raised Atlanta Falcons symbol, moved her fingers along the smooth nylon. She could see T. J. at the ball park, watching the "big boys" practice, getting warm, and taking off the jacket. Probably fussing because he had to keep up with it. Climbing on his bike and heading home with the wadded jacket in his carrier—until it blew out in front of Jeremy Dylan's house.

Why did I let him go? Leah asked herself again. *Why didn't I say "Watch out for cars" instead of "Wear your jacket"?*

The telephone rang out like an alarm. Leah grabbed it on the first ring and said, "Hello!"

"Hello, Leah. It's Mother."

"Mother!"

Leah's parents had retired to Denver, where they had lived when Leah was born. Her father's retirement from IBM coincided with her graduation from Peabody College, and he had said, winking, "You've got your education, and you've got your diamond ring, so I guess we've done our job, and you don't need us any more."

It wasn't true. She suddenly missed them more than she ever had.

"Are you all right?" asked her mother. "You sound a little breathless."

"I'm all right. I'm so glad you called, Mother. How's Dad?"

"Just great. And I have some good news. Laura has a baby boy. They're both doing well, and Russ, too, I ought to say. The baby's just perfect!"

"That's wonderful. I'm so relieved that everything's all right." Leah was suddenly ashamed that she hadn't called or written her sister—hadn't even given a thought to her pregnancy in weeks. Laura was nineteen when T. J. was born, and she had come to help out with him, and had stayed almost a month.

"They named him Thomas Russell, and they're calling him Tommy. Of course, your dad's proud." Leah's mother talked on, like any grandmother. Leah was glad that her parents lived in the same city with this new grandson. They needed him. T. J.'s death had hurt them, too.

"Thomas Russell. I like that." Leah remembered how T. J.'s name had made her dad proud, too. Thomas after Leah's father, Jarrod after Clay's father. Clay had said that Thomas Jarrod Padgett sounded like a statesman, a little heavy to hang on an eight-pound boy. Hence, T. J. "Yes, Tommy's a good name."

As the conversation neared an end, her mother asked, "Are you and Clay going to spend Thanksgiving with his family?"

Leah thought for a moment. "I'm not sure." That had become the tradition, but, so far, she and Clay hadn't talked about it.

"The Padgetts are such a big, warm family. I'd feel a lot better about you if I knew you were with them on Thanksgiving. Unless, of course, you could fly out here."

"There's nothing I'd love more, Mother," said Leah, and she meant it. "But, for a four-day weekend, it's just too long a trip."

"Then we'll talk about it before Christmas. Do take care of yourself, Leah. You sound—I don't know—unwell." It was the kind of word that only her mother would use.

Everybody's a psychiatrist, thought Leah, but she didn't mind it so much in her mother. She wished it were possible to spend some time with her, just to be nothing but her child again for a few days. But there was no point in troubling her, not when they were more than a thousand miles apart. She said, "I'm not *unwell,* Mother. I just need that four-day weekend."

When they said good-bye, Leah quickly returned the red jacket to its place between the sheets in the drawer. Clay mustn't know. He knew about the episodes in the summer, but she had promised after the last time that she would put the jacket away. She would, sometime. She would go into T. J.'s room and put the jacket with all the other clothes. But as long as Clay didn't know where it was. . . .

Pushing against the bottom drawer, Leah thought of something that Mr. Carlton had said at the first of school. He had told her, "Don't expect school to work a miracle for you." But she had. She had counted on school to keep her from remembering, from hurting, from needing the red jacket. It just hadn't worked. Not because of Edward, but because of *her.* She wasn't the same person who had loved each motley crew for ten years. No one understood. Everyone kept trying to reach in and pull out the loving, trusting, levelheaded Leah, and she just wasn't there anymore.

She climbed onto the bed and stretched out flat on her back, reciting softly:

O, it sets my heart a-clickin' like the tickin' of a clock,
When the frost is on the punkin and the fodder's in the shock.

Maybe Clay had been right all along. Maybe she should see a psychiatrist. Maybe she was going crazy.

6

A round of flu swept through Conroe Elementary the first week in November. On Monday attendance was already down, and the school sent sixteen children home during the day. Leah's absentees numbered five on Tuesday, one of those being Edward. On Wednesday Emily was among the absentees, and the class was a sparse eighteen. Leah had often wished for a teacher-pupil ratio like that, but the circumstances made the small class more prohibitive than conducive to learning. The students who had managed to stay clear of the flu seemed to have declared a holiday. They chattered incessantly and took liberties that they knew were not permitted in the course of a normal day, like scurrying across the room to deliver notes. Even when Leah scolded, she was more likely to get a sheepish grin than a repentant, ducked head.

"I didn't finish my homework," said Corey, when Leah gathered up math papers. "I didn't feel too good last night."

"Me neither," said Angela Raskin, a chubby girl with a perpetual pout on her baby face. "I thought I'd prob'ly be sick today anyway."

Even Teresa, who never made less than ninety in spelling, put in an argument for postponing the weekly test. "The others will have to take it when *they* come back, so why can't *we* wait, and just have one test?" Then, gasping with another idea, she actually bounced in her seat. "I know! We could have a spelling bee! Wouldn't that be fun, Mrs. Padgett?"

"Yeah, let's do something fun," Danny offered. Except for one patch of Mercurochrome in the corner of his mouth, no evidence of his bike wreck remained. "Let's play a game. Do you know how to play Spelling Baseball, Mrs. Padgett? We used to play it all the time last year."

The carnival atmosphere was as contagious as the flu, and Leah decided that there was no use fighting it. No one could focus on work, meaning Leah, as well. She postponed the test in favor of a spelling bee. She handed out a choral reading about the Pilgrims, pulled from her files on a sudden impulse, and let the students begin working on the lines. She instigated a general cleanup of the room—washing blackboards and desk tops, cleaning out desks, dusting windowsills—and ended the day with Mrs. Frump on her knee, telling knock-knock jokes.

The children departed on a wave of laughter. Danny left saying, "Thanks for letting us goof off, Mrs. Padgett!" Most of the children were not even carrying books home. Of course, since conferences were scheduled for the next two days, the students wouldn't be coming to school anyway. But they ought to have some work to do over the long weekend, Leah knew. Other students were leaving the building with books, and Leah had intended to make assignments. She had it all in her lesson plan book, for all the good that it did there.

Lisa, who had won the spelling bee, slipped a note into Leah's hand before hurrying out into the hall. "Thank you for having the spelling bee," she had written. "This was my best day of school ever. I love you. Lisa C."

Leah felt a sudden rush of tenderness for the whole group as they brushed by her at the door and turned up faces shining with innocence. They trusted her, without questioning what she was or wasn't. It was enough that she was the teacher. They didn't fill out evaluation forms on her. If she had them study nouns or memorize Shakespeare, or if she had them scrub desks, as far as they were concerned, that was the way it was supposed to be.

She closed the door and started through the room, straightening desks. *What was it all about?* she wondered. It wasn't just surviving that mattered, or even squeezing some joy for herself out of every ordinary day. It was more than keeping her mistakes from Mr. Carlton. Why was it so hard to figure out, this year, what she had taken for granted all the other years? Leah stopped at Lisa's desk. She had to work this thing through, this business of teaching. She had been in it for ten years now because she liked it. Sometimes she had loved it. She had taught because it was satisfying. But when it came down to fundamentals, weren't the *children* the ones who mattered? Education could deliver them from a dead end in the inner city, and she was part of that lifeline. For this year, she *was* their lifeline.

But knowing that only made their trust an accusing finger. It was bad enough that school hadn't worked a miracle for her, but it was worse that she had, so far, cheated her children out of two and a half months of their education.

She clenched her jaws. Why had she let them become important to her? She didn't need this guilt, on top of everything else.

"There's a letter from your mother on the table," Leah told Clay when he came in that evening.

"What did she have to say?" he asked, shuffling through the other mail, mostly bills, to find the letter.

"I didn't read it."

"Why not?" He held the envelope up to the light, and shook the letter down to one end. Then he tore off no more than a fourth of an inch on the other end. It was his own particular way of opening letters. "You're certainly welcome to read anything my mother writes to me."

"Oh, don't make so much of it," Leah said, wearily. "I just haven't had a chance." She slid a pan of rolls into the oven.

Clay read silently the large fancy script, written on two pages of lined tablet paper. Then he folded the pages together and returned them to the envelope. "She didn't have much news. They've already had a light snow. All the family's well."

"Good. I hope her arthritis isn't bothering her too much this fall." Leah was sorry she hadn't read the letter and honestly didn't know why she hadn't. She guessed it had just seemed like too much effort and she had other things on her mind when she brought in the mail, but either was a flimsy excuse.

"She didn't say anything about her arthritis. Mainly, she wanted to know if we were planning to go up there for Thanksgiving." He paused a minute and then asked, "Are we?"

Leah brushed by him with the plates and silverware. "It's up to you," she said. "What do you want to do?"

Clay followed her to the table and helped her arrange silverware. "I'd like to go, but I'm not going to make an issue of it."

"No need to make an issue. We'll go."

Clay seemed to lose his breath for a moment.

"We go every year," Leah told him.

"Fine. We'll go." His surprise worked into a grin. "That was easy enough."

Leah's lips turned up a little at the corners. "I'm not so terribly unreasonable, am I? All right, maybe sometimes I am. But I'm not *intentionally* hard to live with."

Clay took her hands in his. He seemed almost shy, looking down at her fingers. "I know you're not," he said.

She said, "Anyway, I love your family. I'll enjoy going to New Hope as much as you will."

"I hope so." He squeezed her hands. "And you know what I want you to do? I want you to buy yourself four new outfits. One for each day of the trip."

"Four?"

"Sure! You haven't been on a buying spree in a long time."

Leah thought about it for a moment. "I know just the place," she said, "but I'll do well to afford one outfit if it's the sort of shop that I think it is."

"Don't worry so much about the money."

"That doesn't sound like you at all. Come on. I have to make the salad."

As Leah tossed the vegetables in the big wooden bowl, Clay leaned against the counter top and watched. He talked about his mother, about the feast she would prepare at Thanksgiving. He speculated on which brothers and sisters would be there. Leah hadn't seen him so cheerful in a long while. Obviously, a trip to New Hope meant more to him than she'd realized.

After dinner, Clay said again, "When you go shopping, just have a good time. Find something you really like, and buy it."

"You've convinced me," said Leah. "But how about you? Aren't you needing a new suit?"

"I am, and I intend to buy one this weekend."

"Is there some reason for this?" asked Leah. "With all due respect, you've always been a little conservative where money is concerned."

"More than a little conservative, I'd say. But tonight, I'm in exceptionally good spirits. That's all."

"Is it because we're going to New Hope for Thanksgiving?"

"It's because of *you*. Don't you know that?"

Leah hesitated. She didn't like thinking that his moods depended on hers. "No, I guess I didn't."

"Sure, I want to go to New Hope, but what matters is that you were so *agreeable*. And do you realize that this will be the first time we've been anywhere together in months."

She knew what he had started to say: *Since T. J.'s death.* It always came back to that. "The Thanksgiving get-together with your family is a tradition," she said. "I don't deserve a medal for being agreeable about that."

He said, "But it's a beginning."

The evening had been pleasant and relaxing. Leah had been reminded of the days, early in their marriage, when their conversations grew out of the great need simply to share, when they could never get enough of just being together. Tonight they had lingered at the table, nibbling and sipping coffee, and for the first time in a long while, Leah had felt a warmth growing between them. Now, a familiar darkness began to rise like a wall around her. Clay was ready to move on, *get on with their lives—wasn't that how Catherine had put it*? And she wasn't ready. Something in her resisted. Clay kept looking for beginnings, for signs that she was all right. He hung on to every soft word, attached some significance to every smile. Why wouldn't he just give her some space?

"Just take the trip for what it is," she said. "Let's try to enjoy being with your family, without thinking beyond that."

"All right. We'll just take it for what it is," he said. But something in his voice sounded too hopeful.

The next day was an easy one. Only six of Leah's parents showed up for parent-teacher conferences. Leah had hoped to see Edward's mother, but at the end of the day, she had to admit that she was relieved not to have had that conference. It was a pleasure to meet mothers like Mrs. Kirk, a pretty, young black woman in a nurse's uniform, who said, "Teresa just *loves* school. She's not missed a day since she started kindergarten. If she was to say she didn't want to come, I'd know there was something *awful* wrong with her!"

And then there was Lisa Cotham's mother, as freckled as Lisa and even more shy.

"Lisa's an excellent student," Leah told her, "very conscientious, sometimes even a little nervous about her work. She tries hard to please, and she needs a lot of encouragement. I never have any problems with Lisa. My only suggestion is that you try to give her some extra attention, let her know how proud you are of her. Do you see what I mean?"

To which Mrs. Cotham nodded timidly and replied, "I'm glad she's doing all right."

Most of the conferences were brief. Corey's mother was the only parent who lingered, as she digressed from the subject of Corey to the troubles of her three older boys. "Sure, Corey's a little fidgety," she said, "but he's nothin' like Tyrone. Then take Marvin and Joel. They both dropped outa school, and they've brought me nothin' but heartaches. I've said more than a few times that I was through with 'em, but you never can be, not when they're your blood, so you just keep on. That's all you can do."

None of the parents were hostile or argumentative. None had to be told bad news about their children. It was a pressure-free day, the most relaxing day Leah had spent since the beginning of school.

A half hour before the teachers were scheduled to leave, Catherine leaned around the door facing of Leah's room. "Busy?" she asked.

Leah looked up from her lesson plan book. "Not really. Come on in."

Catherine held up a little plastic bag with four chocolate chip cookies in it. "I had these left over from lunch," she said. "I thought you might like to share them with me. They're homemade."

"Sounds wonderful. Pull up a chair."

Catherine glanced at the lesson plan book. "Getting a lot of work done?"

"As a matter of fact, I am. I only had six conferences, so I've had a lot of spare time."

"I like your new bulletin board," Catherine indicated the Pilgrims and Indians feasting in the back of the room.

"Thanks. I put that up today, too."

Catherine nodded approval as she placed a chair at the side of Leah's desk. She said, "It's a shame to have rooms right around the corner from each other and never have a chance to visit."

Leah said, "You're right about that. I'm glad you came."

They eyed each other for a moment, with tentative grins just beneath the surface. Then something connected, and they both laughed.

For a week now, Leah had tried to figure out a way to patch the rift between them, and Catherine had done it with a bag of cookies. That was Catherine for you. Maybe now they could both just forget that morning in the teachers' lounge.

Catherine opened the plastic bag and held it out to Leah. "Eat up," she said.

The air was brisk, and the sun hung low in the sky, casting long shadows. Leah had always wondered just what it was that made autumn such a melancholy time of year, and now, at once, it occurred to her. The shadows, of course. The cold, elongated shadows that fell all around, taking bites out of the sunny day. They mocked you with their disproportionate forms, reminding you that daylight is brief, and the dark hours are long.

Leah felt for her keys as she reached the car, and then, on an impulse, she searched further in her purse, coming up with a business card. *Maggie's Rags, Designer Creations*, she read. That was it. Clay had encouraged her to buy some new clothes, and what better opportunity would she have than now? The easy pace of the day had left her wanting to do something besides go home and crawl into bed. What was it that Mrs. Blake had said, the day she had talked about her daughter's boutique? Leah recalled a piece of the conversation: "Her customers are beautiful young women, like yourself." Leah thought about it for a minute. Maybe it was time to start thinking about new clothes. Clay had insisted, hadn't he? The more she considered Maggie's Rags, the more appealing grew the idea of buying designer fashions. Leah had always been a shrewd shopper, rarely splurging, but as she left the parking lot and headed for Palmer's Square, she had a feeling that this was going to do her a lot of good.

Maggie's Rags looks more like a fine lady's drawing room, Leah thought, *than a dress shop. This may be a little rich for me*, she told herself at first, hesitating at the door, but a tall woman with an ingratiating smile had already seen her. Leah took a deep breath and closed the door behind her. It couldn't hurt to look.

The woman came across the room and greeted Leah. She was slender and poised, with sleek, chestnut-colored hair in a twist at her crown. Leah wasn't sure whether she was actually beautiful, or just so graceful that she presented that illusion.

Leah introduced herself and mentioned Mrs. Blake at Conroe. She wasn't surprised when the woman said, "I'm delighted to meet you, Leah. I'm her daughter, Maggie."

Leah had expected the style and poise. She hadn't expected the easy charm. Maggie Blake might have looked like a high-fashion model, but talking with her was like chatting with a next-door neighbor.

"I hope Mother didn't go on and on about the shop," said Maggie. "Sometimes she does that, and, frankly, it's embarrassing. But maybe it's no worse than grandmothers who brag about their grandchildren, and since Mother has none, I guess I can't fuss about her too much."

Leah smiled. "I seem to remember something mentioned about grandchildren."

"I knew it. She goes on about that subject, too. But I think she's realized that since I'm her only child, grandchildren will be a while in coming." She winked. "Maybe that's why she has so much to say about the shop. She's trying to convince herself that I'm accomplishing *something* in life!"

"I think she's very proud of you," said Leah.

Maggie laughed. "As proud as she can be of a daughter who hasn't produced grandchildren."

A collegiate-type in a jogging suit came in, and Maggie said to Leah, "She's here to pick up a dress. Why don't you pour yourself some tea?" She indicated the sitting area that had caught Leah's attention when she had first opened the door. "I'll only be a minute."

Leah poured tea from a silver teapot. She settled into the plush, pale blue sofa, and ran her finger along the design of the warm cup. With a Persian rug beneath her feet and fragile hand-painted china in her hands, she felt like a lady of distinction. She looked around the room at the paintings—a couple of Monets—the flower arrangements, and the surprisingly few racks of dresses on display. Yes, she'd be lucky to buy *one*, but whatever it cost, it was worth it just to feel so expensive for a few minutes.

Mrs. Blake was right about her daughter. *She does have a flair for this,* thought Leah, as she watched Maggie assist the customer, take two calls, and exchange a few words with a delivery man who brought in a package. She was both personable and professional, the image of success. One of those people who took each crisis in stride. Or maybe she never had a crisis.

"I hope you haven't felt neglected," said Maggie, sweeping back to Leah. "I have an assistant who could have taken care of those little matters, but she's on an errand."

"I've just been enjoying the tea," said Leah, rising to her feet.

"Good. Now, if you're ready to see some of our new fashions, I can think of a dozen outfits that you could do wonders for."

Leah considered that one. It might be a standard line, but Maggie made it sound original, and beyond that, sincere. Maggie Blake certainly knew her business.

An hour later, Maggie folded a silk dress and placed it in a large, flat box. "We'll try to do the alterations on your suit tomorrow," she said, "but just to be sure, why don't you plan to pick it up Monday?"

"Fine," said Leah, taking out her checkbook. She glanced at her balance. She could handle the amount, but it certainly was a chunk. She wasn't used to writing checks like this for clothing.

"You'll be able to wear these clothes for years," said Maggie. "They're classics. Expensive, yes, but in five years you'll tell me you're still getting your money's worth."

It occurred to Leah that she probably ought to be embarrassed, but she wasn't. "Are you psychic?" she asked, and they both laughed.

As Maggie finished writing up the sale, a young woman came into the shop, carrying several hangers of clothes. She said,

"Mrs. Hardaway only took one, the Marquis corkshell and green."

"A good choice," said Maggie, still writing. "Don't worry. She'll be calling us again next month."

The young lady removed her cape and revealed a striking maternity dress. "Have you been busy?" she asked.

"Not terribly." Maggie slid the ticket in front of Leah. "We've had a good time, haven't we, Leah?"

Leah laughed. "Don't ask me that while I'm writing my check."

The young woman, whom Maggie introduced as Rosemary, was charming, much like Maggie. "She's my assistant and right arm," Maggie said, "and I'll be lost when she leaves me after Christmas."

Rosemary patted her stomach. "I'm going into the mother-hood business. I haven't ruled out coming back to work, but for a while I'm sure I'll have a full-time job at home."

"Yes, you'll be busy," said Leah.

"Do you have children, Leah?"

Maggie's question was sudden, like a slap. Leah answered quickly, "No."

"Leah teaches at Conroe, with my mother," Maggie told Rosemary, and then, looking back at Leah, she added, "That's a demanding profession, especially teaching in the inner city. Mother spends hours at night coming up with new ways to motivate her students."

"She's a fine teacher," said Leah. She didn't want to talk any more about herself. Most of her acquaintances thought of her in a certain way, and it was refreshing that Maggie Blake didn't think of her like that.

But Maggie went on. "I'm sure you're just as dedicated. I know I've heard my mother speak of you. In fact," she stopped suddenly, and Leah knew that now she had remembered. "Yes, I'm sure she's mentioned you." Her voice was different now, tempered with sympathy or pity or whatever it was that Leah always seemed to hear in Catherine's voice, in Reverend Kent's, even in Clay's, sometimes. Or could she be imagining it—because *she* could think of herself only in one certain way?

"I'll be back Monday," she said, making a departure that probably seemed abrupt to Maggie and Rosemary, but she couldn't keep up the act any longer. Or was it an act? She had thought she was being herself. But who was that? Every time she thought she knew, she was haunted by the question: Now that she had been T. J.'s mother, could she ever be anyone else?

It was dusk when she arrived home, and the house was dark and chilly. She went through the rooms, flipping on lights, and turned up the thermostat in the hall. She went to the bedroom and set her dress box on a shelf in the closet. Then, as if she had been headed in that direction all along, she went to the chest of drawers and took T. J.'s red jacket out of the bottom drawer.

It was time to put it away. If there was any hope of ever pulling herself together, she had to start there. Maybe she wasn't ready to go through all of his things or to open up his room, but surely she could walk in there and lay the jacket on his bed, and walk out. If she couldn't do that, after all this time, maybe she never would.

She held the jacket against her. Putting it in another room didn't mean she was putting T. J. out of her mind. You just couldn't attach yourself to a piece of nylon. It wasn't healthy. It wasn't sane. She brushed the cool red sleeve against her cheek.

"What are you doing?"

Clay stood in the doorway. He held onto the door facing, looking as if that were all that kept him on his feet.

"I didn't hear you drive up."

"I thought you put that away, a long time ago."

"That's what I was doing. I was putting it away." Leah realized how breathless she sounded, as if she had run a mile.

For a moment, Clay just looked at her. Then he jerked at the knot of his tie and turned away, as if that one motion had sapped the last drop of his strength.

Leah crammed the jacket back into the drawer and slammed it shut.

Clay was sitting on the sofa when Leah came into the den. Just sitting, with his head back, his fingers laced behind his neck.

"You don't believe me, do you?" she asked. He didn't answer. "I was just about to take it into T. J.'s room. But you don't believe me. You think I'm crazy. You think I'm losing my mind."

"I don't think you're crazy," said Clay. "I just don't think you're trying."

"I *am* trying." She sat down on the other end of the sofa. "I bought some new clothes today, expensive clothes. Remember, we talked about it last night."

He let his hands fall to his knees, but he kept looking at the window and beyond the folds of draperies. "I remember last night. I think I said something foolish, to the effect that it was a beginning."

"That wasn't foolish," said Leah.

"I don't know," he said, still talking toward the window. "Sometimes I get a glimpse of hope. I think we can work everything out. And then something happens, like this. . . . "

Don't you know that's how it is with me? That's exactly the way it happens with me. She said, "What can I do?"

"You can let us get on with our lives."

She gave a sarcastic little laugh. "That sounds just like something Catherine said the other day. She's worried about us, too."

"Well, *you* ought to be worried about us, Leah." He finally looked at her. They were silent for a moment, and then, at once, he said, "You know what I was wondering on the way home today? I was wondering if you'd ever want another baby."

"How can you even think of that?" she asked, almost in a whisper.

"I wasn't thinking of this year, or next year. I was thinking *ever.*"

"I can't talk about that yet." Leah turned her head.

Clay leaned toward her. She could feel him there. "Do you see what's happening to us? I've hardly touched you since T. J.'s death."

Leah felt the space between them turn to ice. *This may be the most important conversation of our lives,* she thought, but she didn't feel anything but ice. She stood up and folded her arms. "I don't blame you for being bitter," she said with her back toward him. "You don't understand, and I don't think you *can* understand. Somehow you've managed to get over losing T. J., and I haven't. I can't."

"Do you believe that, Leah?" Clay came around and faced her, looking straight and hard into her eyes. "Do you really believe that I don't hurt for T. J. anymore?"

She felt her throat go dry. Clay's eyes were narrowed, with little crow's feet spreading from the corners. He looked more than tired. He looked weary.

"If you believe that," he said, "then you and I are farther apart than I thought." He grabbed his coat from the arm of a chair, and let it flop over his shoulder.

"Where are you going?" asked Leah.

"I don't know," he said, and the door slammed behind him.

She heard the engine turn. She knew what she should do, but for the life of her, she couldn't move.

7

Leaving the house in the throes of a conflict was a first for Clay. He was compelled to get *out*, but he backed out into the street with no inclination as to what should happen next. He cruised around in the neighborhood for a few minutes. He drove out to a little park where he and T. J. had flown kites and passed from one side to the other by way of a winding gravel road. Then he headed in the only direction that seemed natural for him, toward Arden.

It was such a familiar course that he scarcely had to think about which turns to make. His car knew the way. But as he came to the bypass, abruptly, he took the other route. He turned toward the town proper, avoiding the service stations and all-night markets with their glaring lights, and threaded through narrow streets where the dark stores had closed at five. He drove to the town square, which was all but empty, and pulled around a policeman in a patrol car and someone in a pick-up truck who had met in the street and stopped to chat. He circled the courthouse, past the cafe where a woman was pulling down the shades, and continued out through the old residential area. In the dark the houses were all yellow windows, and Clay imagined that the warm lights spoke of peace and harmony inside. He envied what he believed to be the simplicity of the Arden people's lives. At least it seemed so tonight, just as it had appeared on the morning that he and Carmen had passed this way. He wondered where Carmen lived. In a condominium off the Nashville Highway, she had said. It was just as well, Clay told himself, that he didn't know any more than that.

He was nearing the university when a poster struck his attention. It was tacked to a light pole, and in bold letters were the words: "Community Players Present *Fiddler on the Roof.*" With a glance in his rearview mirror, Clay quickly pulled off on the shoulder and got out of his car. He walked back and read the smaller print on the poster: "October 13 - November 5. Thursday, Friday, Saturday nights. 7:30. Old Capri Theatre, 1220 N. Wilshire." He thought about it just for a moment. He knew what he wanted to do.

The Old Capri was a renovated movie theater, without much renovation at that. Clay was surprised that he had trouble finding a place to park, but he hoped that the crowded parking lot meant a full house. That way, he would be just another dark body in the audience. He didn't want Carmen to see him, but he wanted to see her. Leaving the car, he found himself hurrying, and he felt a ripple of anticipation. It seemed not so long ago that he had seen the same musical at the University of Tennessee, over and over again, every night, until he had memorized most of the lines and all of the songs. He had gone to watch Carmen appear as Tzeitel, Tevye's beautiful young daughter. And the start of every performance had found him as anxious as if he himself were to be on stage.

That was the sort of emotion that he attributed to youth, as he had lost that stir of expectancy long ago. But what he felt now was close enough to make him acknowledge that he didn't know himself, inside out, as well as he had believed. That opened up more possibilities than he was willing to even consider tonight. Right now he just wanted to relish that sense of excitement, because it was so rare.

The box office had already closed, but the door was unlocked and a pleasant young man—probably the theater manager— met him just inside. "We're well into the first act," he said.

"I don't mind," Clay told him, and the man sold him a ticket near the back of the house, which was fine with Clay.

He settled in, and it was easy to become absorbed in the play. The characters were well done for an amateur cast, and if the music lacked the polish of professionalism, the performance didn't suffer. But Carmen didn't appear. She was not Tzeitel or any of the characters. At intermission, Clay remained in his seat and scanned his program. His lips twisted into a half-smile as he read, "Carmen Kennedy, Director." *Naturally,* he thought. After thirteen years, Carmen wouldn't still be playing Tzeitel. People grew, and they changed.

He left before the next act.

Clay was fastening his briefcase when George Kirby came meandering through the muddle of desks, like an old man on a Sunday afternoon stroll. Clay had dismissed class several minutes earlier, and the other students had finally cleared out. Now he knew why George had hung around, shuffling papers and sharpening pencils—in general, trying to look busy.

"Do you need something, George?" Clay picked up his briefcase and came out from behind his desk, a clear indication that he wasn't planning on staying around.

George shrugged. "Not really," he said, and then, "do you have another class now?"

"No, not till this afternoon."

"So you're going to your office?"

"That's right."

"Mind if I walk with you? Or is this a bad time?"

It's not a good one, Clay thought, but he said, "Why not?"

George followed him into the hall and said again, "If it's a bad time, I can catch you later."

Clay realized that he was leading by several steps, and there was no reason for it. He wasn't late for anything and he wasn't in a hurry to get anywhere. He slowed down, matching his own pace to George's lazy stride. "No problem," he said. "How's everything with you?"

"Could be better," George was quick to reply.

Clay waited for him to go on, but he didn't. If George had something to say, he was taking his time getting around to it. Finally Clay asked, "What's going on?"

"I'm moving back to Nashville, back home," said George. "I can't afford the dorm any more. My dad's out of work." He sounded as if something in him had switched to "on" and random thoughts had come spilling out. "I'd get a job myself, but I don't think I could work and keep up my grades. That would mean my scholarship. Besides, I probably couldn't even find part-time work."

"I see," said Clay. Again, he paused, but when George didn't go on, he added, "It's too bad about your father's job. What line of work is he in?"

"He works for a concrete company. He did work for them, that is, for twenty years. Now the company's going out of business."

Clay heard, behind the words, the frustration, the sense of unfairness, the not-understanding-why. "But you are staying in school," he said, trying to put the situation in perspective.

"For now. As long as I can afford it."

"You'll miss the dorm, sure, but staying in school is what matters. We have a lot of commuters."

"It's no big deal, leaving the dorm," said George. "I'm paid up through this quarter, but it's just as well that I don't stay."

They turned the corner next to Clay's office, and Clay reached in his pocket for his key. This time he deliberately kept his silence, waiting for George to elaborate. As they reached the door, George finally said, "You can't study in the dorm, with everybody partying all night. They think you're weird if you even try to study."

Clay began to get the picture. He paused with his hand on the doorknob. It was clear that George had more on his mind, but he had guessed right about the timing. It was a bad time. Clay had managed to get through a terrible night, and he knew he wasn't sharp, but beyond that, he couldn't work up much feeling for George's situation. George had some difficulties, sure, but his problem was that he was a chronic worrier. Clay remembered his mother's expression, *borrowing trouble*.

You take school too seriously.

I take everything seriously.

Clay heard himself say, "Come on in if you like."

"If you're sure you have a minute," said George, following Clay inside.

"I have a minute." Clay motioned for George to sit down, but George shuffled over toward the window instead.

"Man, I never realized how easy high school was," he said with a muffled laugh. "I was in the top ten of my class. Sixth out of three hundred. Oh, I hit the books all right, but it was, well, satisfying. You know? No scholarships or money worries, no trouble studying, no apologies for being a good student."

"Do you have to apologize now for being a good student?" Clay asked, sinking into his swivel chair.

George shifted his weight from one foot to the other. "I don't apologize, but a lot of creeps don't have the faintest idea what school's all about."

"They're probably the ones who won't be back next quarter," said Clay.

George let that sink in for a minute and then nodded. "I guess you're right."

"Freshmen have a lot of adjustments to make," Clay went on. "For some, the freedom of being on their own is the biggest adjustment. They have to learn how to spend their time to the best advantage, and how to set priorities. They have to learn, as you said, what school's all about." He leaned back in his chair. "For other freshmen, the adjustment involves being the little frog in the big pond, as opposed to the big frog in the little pond."

He saw, by the way George squared his jaw, that he had made his point. He tried to lighten up by saying, "Hey, you've got a lot going for you, George. I have to believe that things are going to work out."

Not a muscle relaxed in George's face as he said, "My father's theory is, 'The Lord will provide.'" He was perfectly still. He didn't ask, What about that? but the question was in his eyes.

Clay raised a finger in the air. "There's something to that, George," but before he could go on, there was a bold knock, and Shirley Nettleton leaned around the door.

"Excuse me, Clay," she said in a pronounced Georgia drawl, left over from earlier days when she might have been a rosy-cheeked belle. "Could I disturb you for a minute?" Clay started to rise, but she made a sharp motion for him to sit. "Don't get up! I just have one question. Could you meet with Carson and me in the student center instead of the faculty dining room? It's closer and faster, and I'm extremely pressed for time today."

Clay found himself momentarily at a loss for words. He had completely forgotten the luncheon meeting scheduled with Shirley and Carson Lewis to go over some reports for the curriculum committee. "That's fine, Shirley. Whatever," he stammered.

"Good. I'll drop by Carson's class and check with him, but just plan on the student center unless I get back with you."

Clay fumbled with his desk calendar, which was still opened to yesterday. "Eleven forty-five?"

"That's right. I apologize for my intrusion, young man," she said to George, who had sunk back into the corner by the window.

As the door clicked shut, Clay leaned back again and rubbed his eyes. It bothered him to think that he had given such little attention to the meeting. He was the one who had insisted on going over the reports before the full curriculum committee meeting on Monday. His deliberate, systematic practices, like previewing each day's calendar, had fallen apart this morning, but he wouldn't let that happen again.

"I'll leave now."

George's voice jolted him. He raised up and checked his watch. It was 11:20, and he felt the need to splash some water on his face before the meeting. "Sorry to run you off," he said, as George took a couple of long strides toward the door.

"I'll drop by some other time," said George, with that contrived no-big-deal-man expression.

"Good." Clay was trying to remember where they had left off. As he watched George's exit, his sagging shoulders, his loose-jointed walk, he remembered. George had dangled a bait in front of him, and he was about to go after it. Then Shirley had interrupted, and George had quickly reeled in his line.

Reverend Kent would say it was an opportunity lost, Clay told himself.

The breeze was invigorating, with just enough nip in it to warrant a brisk hike instead of a leisurely walk. As Clay crossed the campus, he was passed by a jogger who had worked up a sweat. *That's a great feeling,* he thought, imagining the prickle of cool air against sweaty skin. He had jogged for a while himself, a few years back, until he sprained an ankle. After the ankle healed, he'd never managed to get back into the routine. But he thought of it, now and then. In fact, just last night. Trying to keep a respectable speed on the interstate, he had wished he were in shape to jog about five miles. It would've made more sense, under the circumstances, to be out pounding the track than to be burning gas.

Last night seemed like a blur now. Clay remembered the drive and the play, but it all could have happened a year ago instead of just the night before. What he remembered too well were the sleepless hours after he was home. It wasn't late when he had come in, but Leah was already in bed, her face to the wall. She was not asleep, he was sure. He had watched her sleep too many times, thinking how lovely she was, twisting and sighing, tousling the covers. Last night the covers were too neatly arranged. Her absolute stillness, her inaudible breathing, were unnatural, more like someone in hiding than one at rest.

Clay had wondered how she could remain motionless that

way. He couldn't get comfortable or stay in one position more than a minute. He was up and down, fidgeting, flinging covers. It reminded him of the night after T. J.'s death, when sleep was nothing more than sinking into nightmarish depths, again and again. At least then Leah's presence was a comfort. He could reach for her hand, and even in her sleep, she would entwine her fingers in his. But last night, they were isolated from each other. He had hoped that she would be waiting for him when he came home, and that he would have the good sense to say, "Let's talk this out, no matter where it takes us." But Leah had taken care of that possibility. She had chosen to remain unreachable. The arm's length between them might as well have been a gulf. And Clay had wrestled with a new fear. The question now seemed to be not how long before their relationship could be restored, but whether, indeed, there was any relationship left to heal.

Now Clay tried to focus his energies toward the meeting with Carson and Shirley. He had made one blunder, forgetting the meeting altogether, and one was too many when people counted on you. As he approached the steps of the student center, he squared his shoulders and inhaled deeply, letting the fresh air sting his nostrils and wash his lungs. In the dark of night, you could explore life's complexities, but you didn't drag your confusion like a chain when you went out into public. You kept your perspective, your momentum, kept your chin up and your head clear, kept on, and on, like riding a bike. Clay had taught T. J. how to ride by putting him on the bike and saying, "Pedal!" "But how do I keep from falling over?" T. J. had wanted to know. Clay told him, "You keep going. That's how!"

The student center was packed, but Carson had managed to claim a small table. "Shirley's getting sandwiches for her and me," he said. "Go on and get your lunch. I'll guard the table."

"I'm not very hungry," said Clay.

"You ought to have a cup of coffee at least," Carson told him. Carson was a paternal sort, whose voice rang with authority. The top of his head was bald and the hair around his ears was in thick blond tufts. That was one of the features that reminded Clay of his father, who had died when he was five. Carson was short, whereas Clay remembered his father as a large, robust man, and Carson's beard was a contrast. Still, there was a resemblance of voice and expression, besides the hair and lack of it, that generated in Clay an unusual regard for Carson.

"All right," said Clay, and he went over to the vending machines. There wasn't much of a crowd in that area, and he was back by the time Shirley returned.

"Thanks for meeting here, both of you," she said in her song-like drawl. "I have thirty minutes." She clicked her digital watch. "Make that twenty-five."

Carson was already spreading some papers in front of him, holding his sandwich on a napkin in his lap to give more room on the table. "I have questionnaires back from five faculty members," he said. "Shirley has four, I believe. That's not the whole department, but we have enough information to compile a preliminary report."

Shirley pulled out her papers, and between bites, added, "Some of the faculty members have definite ideas about changes that ought to be made in our honors program, especially where scholarship students are concerned."

Clay was glad he wasn't trying to eat, with all the shuffling of papers in front of him. The three of them scanned all the questionnaires and talked about the generalizations that could be made from their findings. Carson, who had devoured his sandwich in a half dozen bites, jotted down notes. Clay made a few comments, but for the most part, Carson and Shirley put together the skeleton of the report. When they were finished, Clay gave a little laugh. "I don't think you two really needed any help. You have it all under control."

"To be honest," Shirley said, with elaborate gestures, "there's really no need for you to participate in all the specifics. Now don't misunderstand, Clay, I'm delighted to have you so in-volved, but aren't you imposing too much of a burden on your-self?"

"I think a committee chairman should stay in tune with the process, as much as possible," Clay told her.

Carson said, "I, for one, appreciate your direction, Clay. You have a knack for taking the shortest distance between two points. I'm pleased with what the committee has accomplished, and I think we owe a lot to your leadership."

"It does make our work much easier when the chairman takes his responsibility *so seriously.*" Shirley leaned forward and raised her eyebrows, as if she were about to impart a secret. "I suspect that you're the type, Clay, who takes *everything* seriously."

"Too much so, probably," he said, standing quickly and adding, "now if one or both of you would be kind enough to hold this table, I think I'm ready for a sandwich."

The line at the short-order counter had thinned out. Clay exchanged a few words with one of his students who took his order, and with another who was also waiting for her order. Smelling hamburgers frying on the grill, Clay realized how hungry he was. His appetite had made a comeback in the last twenty minutes. He felt relaxed, satisfied with himself. Work usually had that effect on him. There was something therapeutic about accomplishment—digging into a task, working through it, seeing it complete. He hadn't contributed all that much to the job Shirley and Carson had done, but it was enough to give him a lift. The rest of the day, he told himself, ought to be easy.

Then he went back to his table and found Carmen.

She looked as surprised as he. Shirley, who was gathering up her belongings, didn't seem to notice as she easily took charge. "Carmen Kennedy, Clay Padgett, perhaps you know each other?"

They both mumbled, "Yes, hello."

"Good. Most of our faculty members are acquainted. That's the nice thing about a small college. Clay, Carmen's mother and I went to Georgia State together. Imagine my surprise when I found Lenora's daughter on the staff here." She rose from her chair. "Carson had to leave, and I'm late, too, but I'm glad neither of you will have to eat alone. Enjoy your lunch!" She swept out of view before Clay could get his bearings enough to say good-bye.

But Carmen recovered quickly. "Well!" she said. "What a nice coincidence."

"How are you?" Clay managed.

"Fine. And you?"

"Fine."

"Really? You looked whipped."

Clay laughed. "You never were the master of tact, Carmen."

"But isn't it nice to know someone who will always be completely honest with you?" She said it as a joke, but Clay felt uncomfortable about any kind of answer, so he took a big bite of hamburger and let the question go.

"So what's happening with your curriculum committee?" asked Carmen.

Clay perked up. "We're making progress," he said, instantly at ease with this subject. "We're getting feedback from all the math instructors. Already we've found a few concerns that run throughout the department. For instance, there's a lot of dissatisfaction about our curriculum for honors students." And on he went. He was in his element. Carmen listened attentively, nibbling at her salad.

At one point she stopped Clay to ask, "What do you see as the outcome of all this work?"

Leah had asked a similar question once. She had wanted to know if he really thought the committee was important, and Clay couldn't remember what he had answered. He only remembered that her question had offended him. But Carmen hadn't asked in an accusing or disapproving way. That was the remarkable thing about Carmen. She said what she thought. She asked what she wanted to know. And, if you understood this simplicity about her, you didn't have to feel threatened.

"I hope that eventually improvements will be made in our curriculum," said Clay. "All the changes that are needed won't take place overnight. I know that. But a few may. And maybe a few more changes will be made next year. Even if the administration were to do nothing about the recommendations we make, I wouldn't feel that we had completely wasted our time. At the very least, there will be five instructors in our department who will be more effective because of what we've learned working on this committee."

They went on to compare some of the programs and procedures in dramatic arts to those in math. "We could probably profit from a study of our curriculum, too," said Carmen.

"Every department could." Clay swallowed his last bite of hamburger and said, "I'm so caught up in this committee work that I can't seem to stop when I start talking about it."

"If I weren't interested, I'd let you know. What do you think of Shirley?"

Clay grinned. "I like her. I didn't know her very well until we started working together, but she's a smart lady and a hard worker."

"A real trouper, huh?"

"You might say that. I'll put it this way. I'd rather be on her side than against her. She strikes me as one who could be tough if she had to."

"My mother's a lot like her. I'll bet they were a pair, way back when. Oh, I have to tell you something funny." Carmen's eyes widened as she embarked on the story of how she and Shirley had met. "When I called Mother and told her about my position here, she said, 'I believe an old college friend of mine is in the math department there. Shirley Nettleton—I don't think she's ever married. If you should run into her, tell her you're my daughter. And ask her if she remembers the day we were trying to swim across the lake and she suddenly got a bad case of stomach cramps. Ask her if she remembers how I pulled her out!'"

Carmen went on. "That intrigued me, so I made a point of going by Shirley's office and introducing myself. Sure enough, she knew Mother and was excited about meeting Mother's daughter, and before I could get another word in, she said, 'I want you to ask Lenora if she still remembers the day I saved her life at the lake!'"

They laughed, and Carmen added, "I still don't know the real story. When I saw Mother after that, I told her what Shirley had said. She just smiled a kind of *knowing* smile and said, 'People say hindsight is twenty-twenty, but it's not, you know.'"

Carmen picked at the last of her salad with her fork. "I guess there's a lot of truth in that, don't you think?" She speared an olive and popped it into her mouth.

"I guess so," said Clay.

"You were at the performance last night," Carmen said, suddenly. "I saw you at intermission. You left and didn't come back."

Clay fumbled for an answer. "Yes, that's right," and then, shaking his head in resignation, he said, "you get a kick out of knocking away a person's props, don't you?"

"Is that what I did?"

"You took me by surprise, yes. I thought we were talking about Shirley."

"My mind does follow a course, of sorts," said Carmen, "but probably not a logical one."

"I have trouble keeping up," said Clay.

"Very well. I'll give you directions. Follow me back to the subject of last night's performance. I want to know why you came in the first place, and why you left at intermission. And I'm not going to let you get by without answering." She propped her elbow on the edge of the table and rested her chin on her hand.

"I was at loose ends last night," Clay said before he realized it. Once he had said it, it seemed natural to go on. "I went to the theater on an impulse, and then I decided that I had no business being there, so I left."

"You didn't like us?"

"Oh, the musical was fine. I noticed you were directing it. You did a good job."

"It's fun, and you're trying to change the subject."

"I ought to know better than that."

Carmen smiled. "You think I'm too direct, don't you?"

"Being direct is probably healthy," said Clay. "Probably better for you in the long run than agonizing over the possibility of saying the wrong thing. Even when you have the other person's best interests at heart, being blunt may be kinder than being silent."

"Something tells me that you're talking about yourself now."

"Maybe I am."

"Does that have anything to do with what happened last night?"

Clay smoothed his used napkin and proceeded to fold it into small squares. He said, "For months I've weighed every word before I said it, trying not to add to the pressure Leah's under. But last night I slipped up. All those months finally caught up with me, and I didn't handle it very well." Catching himself, he added, "It's all tied in with losing T. J."

Carmen's voice was kind. "It must have been terrible to lose a child."

"It was," said Clay, "and is. I don't know if Leah will ever get over it."

"How about you? It must be just as hard for you."

"Sure," Clay mused. "I miss T. J. There's hardly an hour in the day that I don't think about him. But now I can think about what a great kid he was without dwelling so much on the whys and what ifs. He was a wonderful kid, bright and energetic, full of mischief. That's what I try to remember. So I guess that's progress." He began to corral the disposable dishes in front of him. "I've said too much."

"Not at all." Carmen leaned forward a little. Her voice was soft. "We go back a long way, right? You don't have to pretend with me, Clay. You don't have to wear a pasted-on smile or be Mr. Nice-Guy. It won't change my opinion of you if you need to unload some of your misery now and then."

Clay picked up his cup and watched the black dregs swirl in the bottom. "I won't deny the misery," he told her, "but I can't unload on you. Not any more than I already have."

"How did I know you would say that?" she laughed, scooting out of her chair.

"Carmen, wait." There was a stern edge to his words that he

hadn't intended. Carmen waited, perfectly still, like a reprimanded child. "Carmen," he said, in a more gentle voice, "I'm looking for something to simplify my life, not more complications. Does that make sense? I'm not as straightforward as you, but that's the best way I know how to say it."

She stood quickly, without smiling. "You put it very well, Dr. Padgett," she said.

The cinnamon smell that greeted Clay at the door was one he identified at once; apple pie, his favorite. Sniffing, he went into the kitchen and found Leah carving a roast. "I got home early, so I decided to fix a decent meal," she said, in a tone that was just short of apologetic.

"Smells good."

She glanced at him for just an instant before turning back to the roast. "It'll be ready in five minutes."

"Fine," said Clay, passing into the den. The meal was a conciliatory gesture, he knew. Leah had been concerned enough to make an effort. That ought to be encouraging. But he was just too depleted to care.

Leah was pleasant at dinner, not particularly talkative, but then neither was Clay. She spoke of the parent-teacher conferences that day and mentioned that she still hadn't met Edward Curtis's mother. She described the clothes that she had bought from Maggie Blake the day before, and asked Clay if he had seen the dress hanging in the closet. He said no, he hadn't noticed. It wasn't necessary, he knew, to go into why he hadn't had a chance to notice, since last night.

He was determined that any mention of last night would have to come from Leah first. She didn't speak of it, and Clay wasn't surprised. It was just as well, he thought. He wasn't up to another confrontation. It was easier to play the *polite* game. A smile here, a compliment there. Your turn, my turn, like a warm-up tennis volley. No attempts to make points. Just keeping the ball in play. It was a game Leah played well, and Clay was catching on fast.

The week before Thanksgiving, Clay heard Leah on the phone with her mother, telling her about their plans for Thanksgiving. When Leah finished, Clay said, "I heard you talking about going to New Hope."

"Yes," she said, "we are going, aren't we?"

"They're expecting us up there, but we hadn't discussed it lately. I didn't know what you had in mind."

"I assumed we were going. That was the plan, wasn't it?"

"That was the plan, and still is, as far as I'm concerned. I wouldn't want to disappoint Mother."

"Neither would I," said Leah, and Clay knew that she meant it.

"I'm glad you still want to go," he said.

"I'm glad *you* still want to go." She settled in a chair and reached for a magazine.

Clay folded up the business section of the newspaper and spread out the sports section. UT had a chance to win the Southeastern Conference. Vanderbilt's best quarterback was out for their last game because of a knee injury. Jackson State had been invited to play a bowl game in Memphis. He read that headline a second time, and he realized that he'd already been through the whole sports section at breakfast.

He stood up, stretching. "I'm going to fix myself some hot chocolate," he said. "Want some?"

"That sounds good," said Leah. "Do you want me to fix it?"

"No, I'll do it."

"OK, thanks." She turned her attention back to her reading.

Clay took a long look at her. She was curled in the chair, sitting on her bare feet, twiddling a strand of dark, shiny hair. The polite game made a certain amount of sense, Clay had to admit. It was a short-term answer for Leah, and perhaps for him, too. At this point, he didn't have it in him to think about the long term.

8

Clay and Leah left Nashville before daylight in order to reach New Hope in time for the big Thanksgiving dinner. Leah slept the first leg of the trip, until they made a breakfast stop. At the restaurant, a truck stop on the Cumberland Plateau, the talk was about snow and the waitresses quizzed every traveler for a weather report or a prediction.

"Two inches in Asheville," one craggy-faced trucker announced in a booming voice as he passed behind Clay, leaving a trail of cold air.

"What's the last you heard about the snow?" another trucker asked one of the waitresses, a plump woman about fifty, with tight curls the color of black shoe polish.

"Four inches by night. You'd better get your rig on toward Houston," she said, turning out a pan of steaming biscuits on a plate in front of him.

The waitress who served Clay and Leah was a pretty girl with a rosy complexion and straight, brown hair. "Just so the snow's gone in time for school to start back Monday," she remarked, pouring the coffee.

"You must like school," Clay commented.

"Oh, I don't go to school!" she said. "It's my first grader. Four days is long enough for him to be at home. By Monday we'll be at each other's throats!"

Clay glanced at Leah and was grateful that she was paying attention to another conversation. "Someone just came in from Virginia," she said, "and he told another man that part of the highway was closed, out of Bristol. I wonder if he meant the Virginia side or the Tennessee side."

"Probably Virginia, being north. We'll be on back roads anyway, and I grew up driving in the snow, remember?"

Good humor hung thick in the room, and Clay found himself caught up in the sport of straining to see the first flurry. Leah had said, initially, "I hope the snow won't give us any trouble," but by the time they left the restaurant, she was saying, "I guess it'll seem more like Thanksgiving with snow."

For a while, they amused themselves by checking out weather reports on the radio. Then, going into Knoxville, the snow came on them at once. Big, wet flakes splattered on the windshield, faster than the wipers could swish them away. Clay had to strain to see the road, and Leah had to watch for the road signs. The snow persisted, but gradually it changed to a drier substance that seemed to envelop the car instead of beating against it. Clay was finally able to settle back and stop squinting. "This isn't too bad now," he said.

"The roads will be icy tonight," said Leah.

"But we'll be in New Hope tonight."

"We ought to be there in another hour."

Clay checked his watch. "If we're not, we'll miss the turkey."

The snow diminished to a fine powder during the last hour. The final segment of the trip took them off the interstate, first on a two-lane highway that wound through the foothills, and finally on a gravel road that climbed up the mountain.

As they pulled onto the gravel road, now white with fresh snow, Clay said, "From here on, we could walk if we had to."

"Walk? It's still five miles, straight up," said Leah.

"Three miles," he corrected her, "and not exactly straight up, but I'm glad we have four-wheel drive on the car. I have walked it before, though, several times."

Leah smiled. "Good. If the car won't make it up the mountain, you can go for help, since you're an experienced mountain climber."

Clay grinned. He'd had some doubts about the trip, but so far it hadn't been bad. Not bad at all.

New Hope was one of those obscure mountain communities with no signs, no town square, and no town to speak of. At one bend in the spiraling road, a post office and two stores formed a gathering place, of sorts, but a traveler could easily pass the spot without knowing he had been in New Hope. The community was not so much a place as it was a situation—forty families or so, scattered in a five-square-mile area, bound by tradition and like values.

There was something exciting about coming home, although New Hope hadn't actually been home for years—seventeen, Clay figured it. The day he had left for the University of Tennessee with a scholarship and a head full of big ideas—and little more—he had let go of New Hope as surely as his mother had let go of him. Clay wasn't a sentimental kind of person, but coming back each year was one occasion that justified a surge of nostalgia.

"I see the Quigleys have added a room," he noted, passing a house covered in depression brick, except for the wood siding on the addition. And, farther up the mountain, "The Armstrongs must have their whole family together today. Look at the cars."

"Not as many cars as we'll find at your mother's house, I'll bet," Leah pointed out.

She was right. They drove up beside the mailbox with the words, "Maxine Padgett," painted in red, and Leah counted seven cars already parked in the vicinity.

"Wonder who else is here," said Clay. "There are only five of us children, and the last I heard, Margie's family wasn't coming."

Leah said, "You're forgetting that some of your nieces and nephews are driving now."

"Which ones?"

"Charlie, for one, and Susannah's children—Phillip, and probably Beth, too. Isn't she sixteen?"

"I can't keep up," said Clay.

As he parked, the door of the frame house opened, and a rush of bodies poured across the porch, down the steps, and out into the snow. It was like a friendly attack: hugs, kisses, handshakes, and hearty pats on the back. A barrage of questions came all at once. How were the roads? Did they have any trouble? Did it snow all the way? What time did they leave Nashville? Clay acknowledged as many as he could by nodding and shaking his head, because words were lost in the chorus of laughter. Somewhere in the midst of it all, his mother emerged, the only one who had taken time to put on a coat. A stout woman with a big smile, Max Padgett sang out, "It's a pretty simple family that doesn't know when to come in out of the snow!" She met Leah first, wrapping one arm around her, and held her other arm out for Clay. Her coat gaped open, showing her red gingham apron, and when Clay hugged her, she smelled of yeast rolls and pumpkin pies and all the other wonderful aromas that he associated with her kitchen, and with her.

The group made its way toward the house, some running and shivering, others paying no more attention to the ankle-deep snow than if it had been grass. "Clay, pitch me your keys!" called his oldest brother, Milburn. "I'll get your bags." Clay tossed the keys, and Milburn caught them just as his six-foot son hit him with a snowball.

The threesome—Clay, his mother, and Leah—huddled together as they tramped through the yard. Max alternated hugging one and then the other. "I was beginning to wonder if you'd had trouble," she said. "I was going to be downright worried if Clay Padgett didn't show up at mealtime!"

"So we're not too late?" Clay asked.

"You're just in time. I was taking the dressing out of the oven when you drove up." She squeezed them both again. "I'm so glad you came. You don't know how glad."

"We wouldn't have missed it," said Clay. He looked at Leah, and she was smiling.

An hour later, Clay sank into one of the living room chairs, holding his middle. "Why do I do this to myself?" he groaned. "There's something about a Thanksgiving dinner that makes me eat till I'm miserable."

"I do it every Sunday when we come over here," said Milburn.

Clay's other brother, Ted, joined them, pulling a footstool up by the fireplace.

"You cold, Ted?" asked Milburn.

"Oh no, I just like a fire," he said. "I wish we had a fireplace in our house. Of course, it's a lot of trouble."

Milburn reached over with the heel of his boot and gave the footstool a bump, so that Ted almost lost his balance. "City fellow!" Milburn laughed. "They don't have fireplaces in Bristol?"

Ted grabbed Milburn's boot and made a show of trying to pull it off. Clay was too content, sprawled in the chair, to do anything but laugh. Here were his brothers—one almost forty-five, the other nearing forty—jostling around much the same way as when they had been ten and fifteen. Charlie, Milburn's gangling seventeen-year-old, entered in on the fun, pulling at his dad's other boot, and it was like seeing Milburn again at that age. In fact, Clay thought as he looked around at the nieces and nephews who were filing in, the Padgetts were remarkable in family likenesses. They were tall, large-boned people with fair skin and light hair, traits that belonged to both of Clay's parents. Of course, Max was graying now, but Clay could remember when her hair was the color of sunlight, when she wore long sleeves and a broad-brimmed hat to the garden to keep her skin untanned. Susannah, Clay's oldest sister who was clearing the dining room table, looked a lot like Max. Clay guessed that they all did, but it was hard to say that they didn't resemble their father, too. He had, after all, been dead almost thirty years. Only

Ted was showing signs of balding, and Clay hoped that he had missed that particular gene.

More unusual than the similarities among Clay and his siblings was the way *their* children had kept the Padgett features. There were Milburn's boys, Charlie and Jay, both as fair as Vikings, although their mother, Christine, was a striking brunette. Ted's wife, Lucy, was a redhead, but only one of their three girls had inherited the freckled arms, and hair that, in a certain light, was more red than strawberry blonde. The other two girls had hair like cornsilk, skin like cream. And of course there had been T. J., who had looked the part of a true Padgett, although Leah's black hair and brown eyes were supposed to be dominant.

Leah. So far, at the family gathering, Leah seemed remarkably at ease. He heard her voice in the dining room. She was asking, "Why couldn't Margie come?"

"They're moving." It was Susannah who answered. "Dave had his orders to be in San Antonio by the first of December. Fort Sam, I think it is. Anyway, they're moving this weekend."

Lucy spoke up. "Doesn't seem like they've been at Fort Sill more than a couple of years."

"That's the army for you," said Susannah.

Clay could see Margie, dragging her straw-haired children across an imaginary map from Oklahoma to South Texas. Eric was the same age as T. J., and they could've passed for brothers. The two of them, along with Margie's girls, were the younger set of grandchildren, just as Clay and Margie had been a kind of second family.

Margie had called at the time of T. J.'s death. "I want to come," she said. "I want to be there, but I'd have to bring Eric, and I think that would be too hard for you and Leah."

T. J. and Eric had been inseparable at family gatherings. "Two peas in a pod," Max said. Soul mates. Maybe it was good that Margie's family was moving this weekend.

"We're not hiring now," someone said. It was Ralph, Susannah's husband, one in-law whose children looked like him. But

Beth and Phillip were not unlike their cousins. If their hair was darker, they were just as tall, built like Padgetts.

Ralph was a foreman at the shoe company in Hampton. "We haven't hired in going on a year," he was saying.

Clay could identify three or four separate conversations when he thought about it, but he was only partly tuned-in. The stuffy room and the heavy meal were taking their toll, and he was feeling the effects of the long trip that had started well before dawn. At some point his eyelids had slipped shut, and now his eyes seemed to be weighted down, as if someone had laid a wet washcloth across them. He felt his body molding itself to the shape of the chair.

Some of the boys were talking about Phillip's car, an old Volkswagen beetle he'd fixed up. Clay remembered seeing it parked outside, shined up like a showroom model. "I needed something to drive back and forth to school," Phillip was telling his cousins. He was commuting to the vocational school in Rutledge, just thirty miles away. Clay had considered going there, or rather, Max had wanted him to go there. That would've been the safe choice, never leaving New Hope, marrying a local girl, raising fair-skinned Padgett children instead of going after advanced degrees, eating Sunday dinner with Max, like Milburn and Susannah and their families. What would've been the outcome if he had made the safe choice? Or was any choice ever safe as long as love had any part?

He felt himself sinking, and a warm river flowing through his body. The only thing that kept him from surrendering to the current was the parade of Padgetts that filed through his subconscious. Something bothered him about the procession. There were his parents, his grandfather (whom he barely remembered, who was an ancient, withered version of his father), his brothers and sisters, and all the Padgett children. But there was no system that he could put his finger on, and they were all so much alike that it confused him. He needed to make sense of this, to put them in some kind of order. He pulled Grandfather out to himself, out in front of the group. His parents came next, and they stood beside Grandfather. He identified Milburn and his boys, who lined up beside the others. Then there was Susannah, and Phillip and Beth came to join her. He was beginning to make some headway, but something still was not right about the Padgett clan. He recognized Ted, but Ted's girls weren't so easy to find. There were three of them, and Clay hadn't been around them enough to remember their faces well. Finally he located them and even tagged them with their names, Christy, Amy, and Sara. He found Margie, and picked out her children, Melissa, Brooke, and Eric. Then there was only one left, himself.

They formed an unbroken line, those who came before him, and those who had come after. All with a certain coloring and bone structure and unseen characteristics as significant as their appearance, the Padgett line.

And Clay realized what had troubled him about this assemblage all along. All of these Padgetts were part of something continuous. They kept on producing their own kind. Their offspring provided an extension of themselves, so that they never really disappeared, even in death. It was true for all of them, except Clay. There was no one to carry on in his place, and he did not believe there ever would be.

Sometime later in the afternoon, Clay felt someone shaking his knee and heard Milburn saying, "Wake up, Sleeping Beauty!" Clay blinked and drew himself up out of his slump, realizing that he had, indeed, been sound asleep.

He shook his head and laughed. "Guess I've really been the life of the party. How long have I been out?"

"Oh, maybe an hour," said Milburn. "We've all just been sitting here listening to you snore."

Christine came up behind Milburn, carrying her purse. "Don't pay any attention to him. That's why we're going home, so he can get his nap. And he *does* snore."

"You're leaving?"

"Yeah, but we'll see you later, maybe in the morning." Milburn threw up his hand and said, "Bye, everybody. Come by the house if you get a chance."

That was one advantage of living close to your family, Clay thought. Good-byes weren't such a big deal.

Some of the kids were leaving, too. Phillip was going to his girlfriend's house, and was getting his share of ribbing about it. Two of Ted's girls were going home with Beth, but Susannah and Ralph weren't ready to leave, so there was some discussion about cars. As it wound up, Milburn offered to drop the girls off at Susannah's house. Clay watched and listened, and found himself smiling. Big families were wholesome. There was always a lot of bustling around, and you got used to operating within the framework of other people, which kept you from focusing too much on yourself.

Clay hoped Leah was enjoying herself, and that the companionship of the other women would be good for her. He heard feminine voices coming from the kitchen, and he decided to check on Leah, just to let her know he hadn't deserted her. Besides, he smelled coffee. If he could find any room for a few swallows, maybe that would wake him up.

The kitchen was cleaned up, and Max, Susannah, and Lucy were sitting around the little table where Max ate most of her meals when she was alone. "Where's Leah?" Clay asked.

"She just went into the bedroom to lie down," said Susannah. "She said her head was hurting."

Clay felt something knot up in his stomach. Leah was doing it again. She wouldn't let herself have a good time; one step forward, one step backward. He should be used to it by now.

Max spoke up. "You took your nap. I guess Leah needed one, too." Her tone was just short of reprimanding.

"We did get an early start." Clay tried not to show that he was annoyed. He reached for a mug and started to pour some coffee, but now he had a sick feeling. He set down the mug. "I think I'm still too full for this. I guess I'll see about Leah."

"She's in the back bedroom, where you put your suitcases," said Max. "Let me know if I can do anything."

The bedroom was dark, not pitch dark, but gray and without a ray of light. The curtains were closed, and Leah was wrapped in a comforter up to her neck, with her face to the wall. Clay could see only her hair, spread out behind her. As he walked over to the bed, he realized that he was afraid, and that he had been afraid for eight months. At any time, Leah could go all to pieces. He never knew what to expect from her, and just when he would begin to relax, something like this would happen. It was like watching T. J. when he was taking his first wobbly steps, following him around, ready to catch him, because he was bound to fall. The thing was, T. J. had a way of getting his lumps, even with someone standing over him. And for all that Clay had tried to protect Leah, he knew that the possibility of a breakdown was still there.

"Leah?" He bent over her and saw that her eyes were closed. "Are you all right?" He gave her a gentle nudge, and she twisted a little, turning toward him. She was squinting, as if looking into a bright light.

"I'm sorry," she said, hoarsely. "I guess I have the flu."

Clay put his hand to her forehead. "You do have a fever," he said.

"I ache all over. I'm sorry, Clay. All the children at school had it, but I thought I'd missed it."

"When did you begin to feel sick?"

"My throat hurt a little this morning, but I didn't start feeling feverish till we were doing dishes."

Clay couldn't help feeling both relieved and ashamed, and that mingled with a sudden tenderness. He tried to smooth out the comforter because he didn't know anything else to do. "Can I get you anything?" he asked.

"No. I took some aspirins."

"Maybe you just need to sleep," he said. Then a grin came to his face. "Do you remember when I brought you home with me to tell the folks that we were engaged, and you spent the weekend sick? It was flu then, too."

"The mountains don't agree with me," she said.

"Well, I married you anyway," he told her. He thought how much she looked like that beautiful girl he had brought home with him that winter. He remembered how fiercely he had loved her, how secure he was in her love for him. He was certain of everything in those days. Nothing would have made him believe that even a tragedy like losing a child could result in what had happened to them. What exactly *had* happened to them? Had their love diminished? He sat down on the bed beside her and brushed a strand of hair out of her face. Her cheeks were flushed. She did look sick, weak, vulnerable. She wasn't drawing away from him. In fact, she seemed glad for him to be there. It was funny, in a way. They both knew how to behave in a situation like this. It was the day-to-day that took its toll. They hadn't stopped loving each other, but they had lost something besides T. J.

"Don't let me ruin your weekend," said Leah. "I know you've been counting on the visit with your family. I'm sorry this happened."

"I'm just sorry you're sick," said Clay, smoothing her hair. And he was.

Friday was Leah's worst day. She stayed in bed, rousing up only when Clay came to feel her forehead, or when Max came with liquids for her to force down. By the next day, she was up most of the time, able to sit at the table and eat a few bites of turkey-noodle casserole. The aching went away with the fever, and by Saturday night, she was packing.

Clay was ready to leave, too. He had enjoyed his family, but now he was looking toward home, and home was Nashville, where he and Leah had a life together. He didn't know whether they could ever find whatever it was that had once made them a unit, long before T. J. But it was worth looking for. He had learned that much here in New Hope.

9

Leah looked at the big, round clock on the back wall of the classroom. It was time for social studies, but the children were reading. They had just returned from the library, and now they were absorbed in their books. Even Edward had his face hidden behind a large "easy reading" book on race cars. *So why bother them?* Leah thought. She had skipped social studies yesterday, but tomorrow, she promised herself, she'd make up for lost time.

Sometimes, when she got off schedule, neglected subjects, forgot to make lesson plans, she imagined that Mr. Carlton somehow knew. Perhaps he sneaked into her room after hours and prowled, studied her lesson plan book, thumbed through the papers on her desk, just to see what was going on. Or maybe he turned on the intercom and listened as she said, "We're not going to have time for social studies today." It was ridiculous, she knew, to think that way, because Mr. Carlton's methods were 100 percent professional. No, it was more likely that he would pass by the room one day when half the students were chattering in their seats and the other half were standing at the window, and he would drop in and ask, "What class is this, Mrs. Padgett?" Or, he would happen to walk in with a visiting administrator who wanted a tour of the school, and her lesson plan book would be open on her desk, showing nothing more than a few page numbers and a word here and there that only she understood. Something like that was bound to happen if she didn't get herself organized. It didn't take a genius of a principal to see that her bulletin boards were still decorated with turkeys and cornucopias, while the other classrooms were all glittering with stars and Santa Clauses. Mr. Carlton would certainly see that, and beyond.

She was still feeling weak from the flu, if that was any excuse. Clay had urged her to stay at home yesterday, but she had said no, the authorities frowned upon teachers who took an extra day after a holiday weekend, whatever the reason. Maybe it was a good sign that she was at least concerned about that sort of thing. She did have a smattering of responsibility, still.

She found a sheet of white paper and began to sketch a Christmas bulletin board for the back of the room.

"Can I go to the bathroom?" It was Danny in front of her desk, doing a little dance on first one foot and then the other. In another child, Edward, for instance, this would mean that the request was urgent. But Danny's fidgeting was as much a part of him as his grin. Leah caught herself staring at him from time to time, and sometimes—scary as it was—sometimes when she thought of T. J., she saw Danny's face. There was such a resemblance. Danny even had a red nylon jacket, though he obviously admired the Houston Oilers instead of the Atlanta Falcons. Leah was glad that it was too cold for that jacket now.

"Can I, Mrs. Padgett?"

She nodded and pointed to the hall pass by the blackboard, the faded piece of laminated cardboard hanging by a piece of yarn from a nail. Danny reached for it and strung the yarn around his neck, prancing off, grinning, with no attempt to hide his delight at getting out of the room.

The hall pass was another reminder that Leah didn't have her act together this year. She had started off every other year with new, brightly decorated hall passes, one for the boys and one for the girls. These leftovers from last year still served the purpose, but why, *why* could she not motivate herself to spruce up this year with the extra touches she had always added before? The plants that she had used in the classroom for at least five years were still at home. And there were the birthdays that had passed without mention. Always before she had celebrated each child's birthday, some years with cookies, sometimes with a card or a little surprise. It didn't have to cost much. The children were overwhelmed by a balloon or a decorative sticker for their notebooks. But this year, birthdays had slipped by without even a chorus of "Happy Birthday."

Mr. Carlton's image flashed across the doorway for an instant, and Leah had to blink. Did she imagine him there, or did he really walk down the hall? Fortunately, he didn't look in the room, if he was there at all.

Emily, who held *Black Beauty* up in front of her, glanced at the clock and then at Leah with an expression somewhere between puzzlement and disgust. Some girls in the back of the room were whispering, and other students began to look up from their books. "We're tired of reading, Mrs. Padgett," someone said at last. She knew it was so. Twenty minutes of silent reading was about the limit for fourth graders. Leah was surprised that Edward's book had held his interest that long. She jotted down in the margin of her lesson plan book: "Edward must like race cars." It was a notation worth entering in the journal she was keeping on him.

"Buddy, will you set up the projector? We're going to see a film on Christmas customs in Mexico." She would squeeze in social studies, after all.

The noise level rose immediately, as students slapped shut their books and slid them into their desks. All except Edward. Even after the lights were out, he kept flipping through his book. He glanced up briefly as a group of brightly dressed dancers whirled on the screen to the lively music of guitars, maracas, and horns. Then he sank back in his seat and propped his book up in front of him.

During her break—or planning period, as most teachers preferred to call it—Leah struck up a conversation with Mrs. Blake in the lounge.

"Is there any improvement with Edward?" Mrs. Blake wanted to know.

"For the last couple of days, yes," said Leah. "I was disappointed that his mother didn't show up at conference time, but I guess that whatever progress we make with Edward is going to have to be without her help."

"That's so often the case. I can't understand the apathy of so many parents, but sometimes we *are* able to make a difference in children, even without their parents' help. I just wish, for your sake, that you wouldn't have had to contend with a situation like this—*this* year."

Leah knew that Mrs. Blake was trying to be kind, but she hated the little intimations that people half-whispered, as if they expected her to open up to them and bare her soul.

"Did Maggie tell you I came to her shop?" she asked quickly.

"Oh. Yes, she did." The change of subject seemed to startle Mrs. Blake, but she got her bearings and went on. "She thoroughly enjoyed meeting you. I got the impression that you two got along very well."

"I think so, yes."

"Sometimes it happens that way. Certain people just respond to each other, you know. I thought, the last time you and I talked, that you and Maggie would like each other."

Leah hadn't given the matter much thought, but now she remembered that, yes, there was an instant liking there, a feeling that she had known Maggie for a long time. She couldn't help being flattered that Maggie had expressed something of the same idea to her mother.

"Maybe Maggie and I could get together sometime," said Leah, actually surprising herself by making the overture.

"I know she'd like that very much, but you'll probably have to wait till after Christmas. She's in somewhat of a bind right now."

"You mean with the Christmas rush?"

"That, and losing Rosemary. Did you meet Rosemary?"

Leah remembered the attractive young assistant. "Yes, she was pregnant."

"That's right, and the doctor has put her to bed. I think she's going to be fine, if she gets her rest, but Maggie was caught unprepared, and I don't know how she's going to manage. She has some college girls that work part time, but they don't really know anything about the business. Maggie says she doesn't have anyone that can take charge, even for an hour, and that means that Maggie is tied to the shop from before ten in the morning till after nine at night. I'm worried about her health. No one can keep up that pace."

She went on, but Leah was only half listening. What she was thinking might be absurd, but it was the first idea she'd had in months that stirred her in any way. She felt a tingle of excitement, a rush of hope. The moment Mrs. Blake left the lounge, Leah went to the phone, looked up the number of Maggie's Rags, and dialed.

"Maggie, this is Leah Padgett," she said, when Maggie came to the phone.

"Leah! How nice to hear from you."

"I'm sure you're busy, so I'll get right to the point. I've been talking with your mother, and she says you're a little short-handed at the shop."

"That's right."

Leah took a deep breath. If she didn't say it now, she would surely back out. "Well, you may be looking for full-time help, and, if that's the case, I'm out of luck, but I was hoping you'd be interested in someone who could work evenings and Saturdays, someone mature enough to handle the shop for short periods of time so that you could at least get out occasionally." There. She had said it.

"Leah! You don't mean you?" Besides the surprise in Maggie's voice, Leah heard delight. "Are *you* interested?"

"Yes, I am. I certainly am."

Maggie laughed. "This is wonderful! How did I get so lucky? Listen, why don't you come by the shop this afternoon, and we'll work out the particulars. You're exactly the sort of person I've been looking for, Leah. Thank you."

"Thank *you*," said Leah. "I'll see you around five."

"Fine."

Leah hung up the phone, thinking, *What have I done?*

Driving home that evening, Leah was still wondering what she had done. She had committed herself to a thirteen-hour workday, five days a week, and had tied up her Saturdays, all without a word to Clay. Of course, she hadn't had a chance to mention it to him, but she would've had a chance if she'd just held back a little. That would be Clay's argument, that she shouldn't have acted on impulse, that this kind of decision ought to involve a lot of thought. Well, if she had thought about it she never would've taken the plunge. Sometimes you could beat an idea into the ground if you thought about it hard enough, and besides that, you could spend all your energies just weighing one side against the other so that once you'd made a decision, you were too worn out to act on it. Maybe she should've talked to Clay first, and maybe she was foolish for assuming this extra responsibility, right on the heels of the flu, but she wasn't sorry. She turned into the driveway and saw Clay's car. She wasn't sorry, she told herself. *You've been waiting for a breakthrough, Clay. Well, maybe this is it.*

Clay met her at the kitchen door. "I was worried," he said.

"I didn't think I'd be this late." She squeezed his wrist. It was a tender sort of gesture, and, at the same time, a plea for support. "I have some news."

Clay shut the door. "Whatever it is, you seem happy about it."

"I am." She felt a little silly, all at once. "Come on. Let's sit down."

"What is it?" Clay was smiling, and Leah realized that he was getting built up for something of monumental proportions. How could her news be anything but a letdown?

Clay took a seat in his big leather chair, but he kept to the edge, elbows on knees. Leah perched on the arm of the couch, and thought how typical it was of both of them, that they could not quite sink back, kick off their shoes, and just chat. Not these days.

She said, "Today an opportunity stared me in the face, and I suddenly found that I was excited about it. I hadn't been excited about anything in so long that I thought I shouldn't let this get by."

Clay listened, nodding. He was with her. She could feel it. She told him about the conversation in the lounge with Mrs. Blake. Then she said, "Something clicked. I guess I didn't consider all the pros or cons, the way you would have, but I just knew all at once what I wanted to do. I called Maggie and told her I wanted a part-time job."

She waited for his reaction, but Clay just looked thoughtful, nodding, with that scholarly air about him. "That's where I've been," Leah went on. "I was at Maggie's shop, finalizing the arrangements. She wants me to start Friday afternoon."

"I see," Clay said, at last. "Well, I guess I should say 'Congratulations' or something. You're obviously pleased with your decision."

He wasn't arguing with her, but his response was short of what she'd hoped for, and she found her own enthusiasm dwindling. "I only promised I'd work through Christmas. We'll just see how it goes."

"That's a good idea. You'll be working a lot of hours and not getting much rest."

"I know, but the shop is so *different* from school that it won't be like working thirteen hours at the same job."

"Thirteen hours." Clay made a little whistle. "I hope you're giving yourself enough time to recover from the flu. You were awfully sick, remember."

"I'll be fine," she assured him. "I feel better right now than I've felt in a long time. Except for tired feet." She kicked off her shoes, but the motion was stilted. Something about this conversation reminded her of the time Clay had come home, burning with satisfaction because he had been asked to serve on the curriculum committee. Now that she thought about it, she guessed she had handled that news badly, though she couldn't say exactly why. Maybe she had felt threatened, and maybe Clay felt threatened now. What was it about them that kept them from getting on the same wave length? she wondered.

"You aren't angry, are you?" she asked. "I probably should've discussed it with you, but I didn't want to be talked out of this."

"Do I look angry?" Clay made a forced little laugh.

"No, and you shouldn't be." She reached down to massage her toes. "You've been wanting me to take some initiative, so now I have, and you ought to be glad."

"Glad's a little strong, but I'm not angry." Clay stood up, glancing at her feet. "You'd better buy some comfortable shoes."

Clay gave a lot of thought to what Leah had said, particularly when he came home Friday evening and she wasn't there. *I feel better than I've felt in a long time,* she had told him, and he was sure it was so. *You've been wanting me to take some initiative, so you ought to be glad.* She was right. Everything she said made sense. If this job could somehow pull her out of the hollow that he could not reach, he should be more than grateful. Looking at the logic of the situation, he told himself that warmed-over lasagna was a small price to pay.

Ben Anderson had called him last Sunday night about helping with a Christmas project for the college and career group from church. They were planning to take some children from poor families on a Christmas shopping outing this Saturday, and they

115

needed help with transportation. Ben's timing was just wrong, Clay guessed, because he had barely walked in the door after the trip to New Hope, and he was so wiped out that he wondered if maybe he was getting Leah's flu. Anyway, he had said something like, "If you can get enough cars without me, Ben, I'd like to beg off this time. I just can't commit myself for Saturday, right now." Ben, of course, had said, "Fine," they'd get enough cars, not to worry. That was what everybody liked about Ben Anderson. He was easy going, never ruffled, the most pleasant kind of guy you could ever want to know.

But tonight Clay thought of the outing for the kids, and it sounded like a worthwhile project, one he'd like to support. As it had turned out, his Saturday wasn't tied up at all. So when he finished the ice cream on a stick that he'd dug out of the freezer, he called Ben.

"You just caught me," Ben said in a loud, cheerful voice. "Catherine and I are going to eat out and take in a movie."

"Sounds good, and I don't want to make you late. I just wanted to tell you that if you still need a car tomorrow for the Christmas shopping, I can help."

"Great! We were going to be crowded with the eight cars we'd lined up, because more college kids decided to go than I'd counted on, and they happened to be kids without cars. We can use you, for sure."

"Good." They settled on the time and meeting place, and then Clay added, for some reason he wasn't even sure of, "I guess you knew that Leah has taken a part-time job at a dress shop during Christmas holidays, so she'll be working."

"Catherine mentioned that. She said Leah was in high spirits, talking about the job. Maybe it'll be good for her."

"Yeah, well, I hope so. I'll let you go now. Enjoy yourselves at the movie."

"Thanks. And thanks for tomorrow, too. And listen, Clay, tell Leah hello for me. It's been too long since we had a Rook game. Tell her I asked about her, will you?"

"Sure. I appreciate it, Ben. She needs friends. She needs to get out, but I haven't had much luck persuading her." He caught himself and was a little embarrassed at the way he'd started to ramble. "Anyway, I'll tell her."

"Well, she's gonna be getting out more now, seeing people in the dress shop. Maybe this will be what you've both wanted." Ben's voice was strong and encouraging, and Clay wondered why he couldn't feel more optimistic himself, for the both of them.

"Maybe," he said.

Catherine's new sweater was pale pink—her color—and as soft as air on her skin. She wondered how many little goats had given their fine wool for her first cashmere sweater. She'd told Ben she hoped they hadn't minded too much. What she really hoped was that cashmere no longer came from goats. That would make her enjoy her sweater more than anything.

The sweater was a birthday present from Ben, a couple of weeks ago. Ben's tastes were improving; his tastes, and their bank account. It was true. Somehow, by just plodding along all these years, they had managed to store up quite a reserve. Not that either of them had chosen lucrative professions. Teachers' salaries were modest, at best. Even Catherine's Aunt Harriet, who had raised her, had known that much. "If you're bound to be a teacher," Aunt Harriet had said, "you'd better set out to marry for money." Then she'd added, in a confidential tone, "They say it's as easy to love a rich man as it is to love a poor one. I wouldn't know, of course."

Well, Catherine thought, she was bound to be a schoolteacher. She had headed in that direction in the seventh grade when she wrote an essay with the uninspired title, "My Goals." "I want to be a teacher because I know how to handle children," she had written. That was probably a good reason, and she wrote the truth. Even at age thirteen, she was the most sought after baby-sitter in the whole town of Coreen, population eleven hundred.

But another reason had come into play two years later. Scottie Hamlin, the brattiest kid in Coreen, finally learned his multiplication tables one snowy evening because Catherine had him line up clothespins in the middle of the cold linoleum floor. Six rows of two, five rows of four, four rows of five. That was all there was to it. How could he have missed something so simple for three, going on four, years? Multiplication was just plain common sense.

Scottie had never seen it that way before. "Yeah, I get it!" he said, and without losing a beat, "so teach me division now."

In the mirror, Catherine saw the corners of her mouth turn up, as she brushed her hair with short, brisk strokes. She couldn't help smiling whenever she thought of Scottie Hamlin. After Scottie, there was no turning back. She had flipped a switch in someone's mind. That was all the power she ever wanted or needed, and money had nothing to do with it.

She hadn't married for money, either.

Ben always said he was a pilot because that was all he knew. That was what he'd learned in the Marines, and he figured he ought to take advantage of it. But once, when a friend had urged him to get his realtor's license, Ben had stated outright, "I'm doing exactly what I want to do, and that's to fly."

He was not a man of eloquent speeches, but he spoke to Catherine of winding rivers and patchwork fields, and he told her of a recurring dream in which he was falling, tumbling through the clouds, but never landing, and never afraid. He always woke from that dream, exhilarated, saying that someday man would fly, not in a plane or a glider, not bound with any kind of attachments. Man would fly, just by looking skyward, maybe raising his arms, and lifting off, soaring with the wind current. "If it doesn't happen before I die," Ben had said, "I hope that's how my spirit goes to meet my Maker."

Ben had made good money after the Marines, flying for commercial airlines, but that had lasted less than two years. It was during that time that they had married, vowed to share their lives with each other, and then found that they went for days without sharing a meal. Catherine made it a point not to complain, because, after all, hadn't she known what kind of schedule she was marrying? But Ben figured that marriage wasn't worth the price of the license if you couldn't drink your morning coffee with the woman you loved, if you couldn't watch the ten o'clock news with her, and hold her in your arms when you went to sleep. That was what he told her. When an opening came up for a pilot with a charter flying service, Ben used every connection he had and took a big pay cut to get what turned out to be a job tailor-made for him. Besides being home most nights, he liked the personal contact with his passengers. "You start out in a six-seater, talking about weather and politics," Ben put it, "but after three hours jammed in there together, you're telling your wife's dress size and showing the hole in your sock."

Flying may have been all Ben knew, but Catherine had figured out a long time ago that her husband's motives weren't far from hers. Money was never the biggest consideration.

That was why their prosperity, in dollar terms, was so amusing. There they were, a fourth grade teacher and a pilot for a small flying service, "sitting pretty," as people used to say in North Dakota, and not caring too much about financial gain. It was absurd, really, when you thought about all the people who ought to be so well off. People with exceptional business sense who suffered one bad break after another. People who clawed for every dollar and wound up with ulcers for their reward. People whose self-esteem hinged on their bank statement.

"What's taking you so long?" Ben's voice, and his image, appearing behind hers in the mirror, startled Catherine. She hadn't even realized he was in the room.

"I guess I'm just piddling," she said. "Piddling, and thinking."

"About what?"

"About our finances. About how little we started with, and how much we've accumulated."

Ben laughed and plopped onto the bed. "You make it sound

like we're big wheeler-dealers. We've just worked hard and saved as much as we could, that's all. Our deposits never have been large, but they've been regular. We've been saving for a long time."

"I guess there's not much else to do with money but save it," said Catherine, "when you don't have extravagant tastes, expensive habits, or children."

Maybe she sounded a little wistful. Ben raised up. "Now you're not going to worry about that tonight, I hope," he said, getting to his feet. "You're supposed to have your mind set on a good meal and a funny movie."

"No, I'm not worrying. I'm not going to let this thing drag me down into the pits. I've seen enough of that with Leah." What she heard in her voice made her think of the Little Engine That Could, puffing away, "I think I can, I think I can!" and she added, with less force, "I'm not being judgmental. Really. I'm just saying that I've seen where Leah's been for these past months, and I pray that I won't ever be there."

"That reminds me," said Ben, "Clay called, and he wants to help us tomorrow. I told him we could sure use him. I guess he's going to have a lot of spare time, now that Leah's working evenings and Saturdays."

Catherine sprayed a whiff of perfume on her neck. "I hope Leah's made the right move. I hope this job will do something for her that nobody has been able to do so far."

"Clay said something like that, too. Come on. Let's go." Ben swung his arm around her shoulder. "Hey, this sweater feels good. I guess I made a good choice."

"Just think of all the people who scrimp and save for their children's college educations, who never get to buy cashmere sweaters."

Catherine said it in a teasing way, but Ben stopped, all at once. He stood her against the door facing, leaned close to her and said, "You've got to quit this. You say you're not worrying about it, but I know you are, and it's something we've just got to accept. If we can't have children, that's just the way it's supposed to be."

"I'm not giving up," she said.

"It's not going to happen, Catherine. We've been married fourteen years. Why should it happen after all this time?"

"I've only been seeing Dr. Albiar for a year, though, and you know what he says. *He finds no reason why I can't get pregnant.*" She made each word fall like a brick.

"He hasn't found any reason yet, but he hasn't made you any promises, either."

"I can still hope, can't I?"

Ben gave her a hard look. Then he shook his head and laughed. "If stubbornness has anything to do with it. . . . " He grabbed her hand. "Come on, let's get out of here."

Saturday morning when the downtown stores opened for business, Ben's entourage of forty children and eleven college students were among the swarms of shoppers who pressed through the doors. Earlier, in the cars, the college kids, who were each in charge of a small group, had set the ground rules for the shopping event. Now they were responsible for herding the children, helping them to choose gifts for their family members, and purchasing the items. Ben and Catherine wound through the aisles, offering assistance, but the college students seemed to have the situation well under control.

Clay chose to be a watcher. He watched the little girl with stringy blonde hair, whose Sunday dress hung at the shoulders and sagged below her knees. His eyes followed her as she meandered through the toys, looking, but never touching, until she came to the aisle with glassy-eyed dolls peering from both sides. She paused and made a sweeping look. Then, like a mother who had spotted a lost child, she went straight to one certain doll. It could have been a live infant, the way she touched the plastic arm, so very gently. It was not the biggest or most expensive doll on the shelves. This particular kind wasn't even in a box, which was a good indication that it was one of the cheaper brands. But the little girl looked at no other. She carefully took the doll from the shelf, hugged it, and went up to the young man who was in charge of her group.

"Can I buy this for my little sister?" she asked, in a tinkling voice.

He gave her a playful scowl. "For your little sister?"

Something bold and determined slipped into her voice as she said, "Yes, for Susan."

The young man cupped his hand around her chin and said, "Gina, your little sister isn't more than a month old. She's not big enough for a doll like this."

"Please, Andy." It was not a whine, but an urgent plea, as an adult might say, *More depends on this than you realize.*

Catherine, who had also been watching, joined the two. "How's your shopping?" she asked.

Andy gave her an exasperated look. "Gina wants to buy the doll for her baby sister, who is *a month old.* I was trying to convince her to choose something else—you know, something that's made for babies."

Gina tugged at Catherine's arm. "I had a Betty Sue before my brother tore her head off." Her voice started to quiver. "I just *know* Susan would like her!"

Catherine and Andy exchanged looks. Andy shrugged and said, "Yeah, I guess she would. Come on. Let's go find a gift for your mom."

Clay watched them as they headed toward housewares. Gina was cradling her baby, and every few steps, she broke into a little skip. Clay grinned. *You've got a good mother, Betty Sue.*

He watched the children who held back, their mouths gaping, awed by the scale and scope of the expedition. He watched those who dashed from aisle to aisle, examining every object on a shelf in the space of two minutes. They would remember this morning, all of them. Whatever shape their lives took, they would remember that once, in the name of Christ and his love, someone gave them Christmas.

Christmas—Clay had put it off as long as he could. His concept of the time of year had crystallized around exams, after which, naturally, holidays would follow, but he had kept the holiday season at a distance. Until this morning. Until the bell ringer in a Salvation Army uniform held out her cup, and her companions raised their instruments in the brilliant, brass-coated harmony of "Joy to the World." You couldn't delay the Christmas season after that.

And along with the decorations and carols came the gifts. It was time to think of those, Clay realized, and here, this morning, he had a good opportunity. He walked away from the toys. That was the section he always enjoyed most, but this year, he wouldn't be buying toys.

He was leaning on the glass case at the jewelry counter, viewing gold chains, when he heard someone call his name. "Christmas shopping?" asked George Kirby, ramming his hands into the pockets of his army fatigues.

Clay, who had often held back a sigh when George cornered him, met him now with a warm greeting. He was developing a real liking for the young man, and a genuine concern for him, too. George had latched onto him at school in a way that was confining. But here, away from the campus, running into George gave Clay a certain satisfaction, like the unexpected pleasure of seeing an old friend.

"I may shop a little," said Clay, "but mostly I'm looking. Getting my first dose of the Christmas spirit. How about you?"

"Yeah, just hanging around, I guess. I brought my mom to work. She's got a job here as a saleslady. They hired her just through Christmas, but she's hoping they'll keep her on after that, at least till my dad finds something to do."

Clay thought of Leah. "My wife's working during Christmas, too, in a shop at Palmer's Square. Part time, that is. She's a teacher, but, of course school will soon be out for the holidays."

"Where does she teach?" asked George.

"Conroe Elementary, here in Nashville, fourth grade."

"So you're both teachers. I guess that makes it nice."

Not necessarily, Clay wanted to say. It was comfortable talking to George this morning, maybe because Clay was just hanging around, too. He and George had a lot in common. He had known it for a long time. He often saw in George the young man he had almost been. But they were also teacher and student, and Clay was the teacher, so he said simply, "It has its advantages. We have similar schedules, for one thing."

He was glad that a wiry-haired little boy interrupted them at that point. The boy was one of the children who had come in Clay's car, and now he turned up his shining eyes to Clay and asked, "Hey, Mister, can I buy this for my daddy?" He was pointing to a digital watch inside the glass case.

Clay grinned at him. "You'd better find your group, fellow. They're probably looking for you."

"I'm not lost," the boy said, indignantly. "I'm trying to decide whether to buy my daddy this watch or a tie."

"I'd go for the tie," said Clay. "A watch may be a little expensive."

"Would you like for your son to get you a tie?" he asked.

"Yes," said Clay, "if I had a son, and he gave me a tie for Christmas, I'd like it very much. Now you'd better get back to Pam." He saw the group leader a few aisles over, and pointed the boy in her direction.

George was amused. "What was that all about?"

Clay told him about the shopping trip for the children who wouldn't, otherwise, be able to buy gifts for their families. He told him about the little girl and the doll, and perhaps it was that incident that touched George somehow. George nodded, thoughtfully, and said, "Sounds like a real generous thing that you're doing."

"I'm not doing anything but driving a car," said Clay. "It's our church. Our people were the generous ones, contributing to this, and the college kids have done all the organizing. The one guy who's most responsible is a man named Ben Anderson. You'd like him."

"I didn't know churches did stuff like this," George mused. "This is something worthwhile. I mean, you can talk all day about being good Samaritans. I used to hear a lot of *talk* in Sunday School. But I guess you and your church mean what you say." He glanced over at the little boy who was back with his group, examining ties. "This will probably be the biggest Christmas these kids have ever had."

For the first time Clay saw George, not as a student demanding reassurance and emotional support, but as a young man with the potential of giving back the same. That was something that George didn't know about himself. The loner and the cynic was all wrapping. Clay had surmised as much all along, but now he knew. He did not know what would surface as George became a man, but that was part of the mystery and beauty of life.

He thought of the banquet that he and Leah had attended a couple of years ago when they were working with the college and career group. Reverend Kent had spoken to the group, charged them, so to speak, and Clay remembered well what his text had been. He had used the Scripture in Exodus, in which God sent Moses to deliver Israel. Moses was reluctant, unsure of himself, doubtful that even God could transform him into one who could be used for such a mighty purpose. Then God told him to cast his rod on the ground, and when he did, it became a serpent. God told him to pick up the serpent by the tail, and when he did, it became a rod again. "Now therefore go," God said, "and I will be with thy mouth, and teach thee what thou shalt say."

Reverend Kent had put it like this: "God has a purpose for you, and that purpose is beyond your most magnificent dreams. You may be a 'slow of tongue,'" as Moses was. You may have any number of good reasons why God can't use you. But you and I reason in finite, human terms. If we had a way of knowing the maximum that God could accomplish through us, if we let him, it would make us tremble."

Potential. George knew about the good Samaritan. Clay wondered if he knew about Moses.

"George," Clay said suddenly, "why don't you come to church with me sometime?"

George looked surprised, and then he laughed. "I guess you think I could use a shot of religion."

"That's not it at all. I think you've got a lot to offer."

George thought about it for a moment and said, "Well, I guess you could give me directions to get there, just in case."

George did show up at the Sunday morning service.

When Clay entered the vestibule, George was there, wearing a sport coat and tie. Clay wouldn't have recognized him except for his coppery hair, frizzing just above the rest of the crowd. As Clay made his way toward George, he saw that Ben Anderson had already greeted him, and, in fact, Ben already had George smiling.

"Clay, I'm glad to see you!" said Ben. "I want you to meet George Kirby. George, meet Clay Padgett."

"I'm glad you could join us," said Clay.

"Thanks."

They shook hands, both of them grinning. Ben looked a little confused. Clay knew that Ben was the sort of person who could appreciate a joke on himself as easily as he could on the next guy. So Clay went on, saying, "I guess you're on your way to the choir, Ben. I'll be happy for George to sit with me." He turned to George and added, "If you'd like to."

"Fine."

"Good. That's good. Well, I'll see you, George. I'll be in touch." Ben still had a funny look as he left.

"I guess you knew what you were doing," said George.

"Don't worry. I'll set him straight, and he'll get a good laugh," said Clay. "Ben Anderson is probably the finest man I know, George."

They went into the sanctuary, looking for a seat, and Clay whispered, "Any preference?"

George answered in a hoarse whisper, "Back row."

So they sat on the back row. When the congregation sang, Clay was a little surprised that George joined in. He had a rich, baritone voice, and he knew every hymn.

10

The blue spruce that Maggie Blake had chosen was an elegant tree. Situated in the center of the shop, it was straight and full, layered with delicate branches, breathing into the room the fragrance of Christmas.

Maggie held to a theory, which she imparted to Leah: *less is more, and more is too much.* "Take jewelry," she explained. "A few well-chosen accessories are fine; beyond that, you're bordering on gaudy. The classic dress with simple lines is always in good taste. Get carried away with bows or ruffles or buttons and you're moving toward faddish, and, finally, toward tacky. *Less* is the look of a well-dressed woman."

So it was with Maggie's Christmas tree. It was trimmed in thin strands of gold tinsel and small lights with clear bulbs, so that the gold filaments glowed. A single angel of cut glass posed atop the tree, within inches of the ceiling.

As for other indications of Christmas in the shop, there were few of the traditional trappings. Beneath the tree, a half dozen boxes were wrapped in expensive paper and tied with oversized bows, so that your imagination connected with French perfume and diamond earrings, even though you knew the contents to be tissue paper. A cheery holly wreath hung on the door, and that was the extent of seasonal decorations in Maggie's Rags.

And yet, the air was charged with Christmas. There was a wonderful sense of holiday as customers selected party clothes for themselves and gifts for others. They came with money to spend, not looking for bargains, and they spent their money with relish, like gourmets feasting on a fine meal.

Whenever Leah thought of the bustling crowds in department stores, of the long lines and short tempers, she dreaded the shopping that awaited her. She wished she could spend this Christmas season without even entering another store, but, of course, she couldn't buy all her gifts here. She might find something affordable for her mother, but for Clay and her students, and for the family members, she would have to leave the safe boundaries of Maggie's Rags. She thought of all the colored lights and the Santa Clauses, the glitter and the fake snow, and the strains of Bing Crosby's "White Christmas" flooding the stores, and she told herself that it was too much. It was the *more* that was *too much*, just as Maggie had said. And she focused on Maggie's understated, magnificent tree, comfortable in knowing that Christmas could come to Maggie's Rags, fill every corner, without touching her. Here, there were no reminders of traditional, family holidays. Sometimes there were hardly any reminders that she was Leah Padgett, and it was wonderful.

Closing time stretched to 9:45 before the last customer left the shop. Maggie's Rags was not the kind of place that swarmed with shoppers, but those who came generally came to buy. Mrs. Carradine had left with three outfits, totaling nearly a thousand dollars. You didn't say to a woman like that, "It's nine o'clock. We have to close now."

Maggie locked the door and said, "Leah, you're marvelous. That lady has been buying her clothes here ever since I opened, and I've never known her to buy more than one outfit at a time. She's *very* frugal."

"Oh, well, it's Christmas time." Leah grinned. "You said yourself that good clothes are a wise investment, or something to that effect. So that's what I told her. And the clothes we finally chose were perfect for her professional image. She just became a partner in her firm. I'm sure that's the reason for the buying spree. She's a tax attorney. Did you know her firm does business with your father's bank?"

Maggie laughed, and it occurred to Leah that she did sound a little bubbly. "No, I didn't know that," Maggie said. "I did remember that she held a very responsible position, but it's hard to keep all the customers straight. Hard for *me*. I'll bet *you* could give me a life history on everyone you've met since you've been here."

"Maybe, but I haven't met that many. I've only worked a week, for a few hours each day." She wondered, suddenly, if Maggie was gently hinting. Their relationship couldn't have been better so far, and she didn't want anything to spoil that, so she said, "If I shouldn't be dealing with the customers on such familiar terms, please tell me, Maggie. You're the business-woman, and you know the right approach."

"I try to avoid coaching employees as long as they're ringing up thousand dollar sales." Maggie winked. "Believe me, I don't hesitate to offer a suggestion, a mild scolding, or a tongue-lashing, if necessary. You're doing fine, Leah."

"I'm glad." Leah thought, for some reason, of Lisa Cotham and the way her freckles seemed to take life whenever Leah said to her, "You're doing fine." Lisa needed praise, like bread and water, and it was easy enough to condense her into one word: *Insecure*. Leah didn't think of herself that way, but Maggie's approval did matter. *Conscientious*. That was the word. Not insecure, she was just conscientious. Everybody needs encour-agement in one way or the other, she told herself.

"Do you have time for a cup of spiced tea, or do you need to get home?" asked Maggie. She and Becky, one of the part-time girls, had finished closing out while Leah was with Mrs. Carradine, and Becky had left before nine-thirty. "Don't stay unless you want to. I realize that you've put in a longer day than I have."

"A cup of tea sounds nice," said Leah. "Tomorrow's Saturday, and I don't come in until noon. I'll get my rest."

"You're not absolutely exhausted?"

"Not at all. I don't feel as tired now as I did when I left school this afternoon." She followed Maggie to the back, into the area off of the stock room that served as an office. It wasn't decorated in keeping with the rest of the shop, but the carpet was thick, and the furnishings included two wing chairs and a coffee table, in addition to the desk and cabinet of dark wood, and the file drawers. The wallpaper was a pattern of tiny bluebells. It was a pleasant room, one that made you want to linger. "I'll make the tea," Leah offered.

"You're on," said Maggie, easing into one of the chairs. "The spiced tea mix is in the blue-flowered canister.

Leah used the automatic coffee maker to heat the water, while she spooned the mix into thin china cups. Even here, in the back of the shop, you didn't find Styrofoam cups or plastic spoons. Leah thought of Mr. Carlton's shabby office and wished for him a place like this, surroundings befitting his position and his appearance. She thought of Clay's office, which she had visited a few times, drab and uninspiring except maybe for the rows of thick books that never quite seemed to belong in the metal bookshelves. And the offices that had been her father's, through the years at IBM, were as sterile as hospital rooms. Leah had never known that an office could be a cozy hideaway.

When she thought about it, she realized that actually she'd never had much contact with people like Maggie Blake. Not close contact, anyway. She'd been acquainted with some whose life-styles hinted of affluence—she'd had a roommate at Peabody whose parents vacationed in Europe—but it had always been easy to dismiss those, for one reason or another. Her roommate's parents were shallow and pretentious. Her father's boss, who had a summer home on Long Island, was sixty and in bad health. But here was Maggie Blake, attractive, successful, living the good life, and not only was she a person Leah could admire, but one with whom she could relate. Through Maggie, Leah was able to taste a little glamour, too, and it was more appealing than she had imagined. *Yes, you could get used to the good life,* she thought, making herself comfortable in the other big chair.

"You've been here a week, Leah," said Maggie. "I hope our arrangement is working out as well for you as it is for me. I honestly don't know how I would have survived Christmas without you."

"You would've found someone. But," she smiled, "I'm glad it happened to be me. I'm thrilled with my job. Really, it's the most exciting thing I've done in a long time."

"How about school? I mean, do you have enough time to do your planning for your classes?"

"I get everything done on my planning period during the day." She looked into her teacup and said, after a moment, "The truth is, I haven't been bringing work home all year. I can't muster up the same enthusiasm for school that I've had before, and it's frustrating. I needed something like this job to get me out of my rut."

"I've heard a lot about teacher burnout," Maggie said.

"Maybe that's it." Maybe it was, she thought. The way Maggie said "teacher burnout" made it sound acceptable, a malady that could affect any teacher. *Burnout.* A harmless word, like chicken pox. You might be hesitant to talk about leprosy in your family, but there was no stigma attached to chicken pox.

"Teachers in inner-city schools seem to be most susceptible," said Maggie, thoughtfully. "It makes sense. You have to have an incentive to keep on in any line of work. Something besides money, too. If you're teaching bright children, you see a lot of progress from the beginning to the end of the year, and that's gratifying. But when the children have so many strikes against them to start with, progress is slow. Rewards are few and far between." She looked surprised, all at once, as if she couldn't believe herself. "Why am I telling *you* all of this?" She laughed. "I'd probably be offended if you tried to tell me what colors are good this season."

"Well, I might try," said Leah, "if my mother was in the same business as you, and if I'd listened to her as much as you've probably listened to Mrs. Blake."

"That's it, all right," said Maggie. "I grew up with teacher talk. I even thought about being a teacher myself, at one point."

"You're joking!"

"Not at all. Would I have been *that* awful?"

"Oh *no*." Leah rushed with the answer. "That wasn't what I meant *at all*."

Maggie held up a quieting hand. "It's all right, because I know I *would* have been awful. I admire teachers, just as I admire mothers. But I'm too selfish to be either. I don't apologize for it, but it's true. I'm selfish. Maybe it's the only child syndrome. Whatever the reason behind it, I've always put my own needs and wants above everyone else's, and I don't necessarily think that's bad, but it certainly isn't a good quality for someone who deals with children. Or for a wife, either, for that matter."

Leah's first impulse was to rush in again and say *No, no, you aren't selfish at all!* But she caught a note in Maggie's voice that she hadn't heard before—arrogance, perhaps—something that made her hesitate. Then Maggie turned to her and asked, straight out, "Isn't that what marriage is about? Putting someone else first?"

Leah was taken back a little, but she said, "That's not exactly a question for yes or no. It's more complicated than that."

"What do you mean?"

Well, Leah, here's your chance to air your views on marriage. Go to it, girl. It was almost comical. Who was she to say anything about marriage, when hers was delicately balanced on the edge of a cliff? She said, "Sometimes you don't mind putting someone else first. It isn't always sacrificing. You can even get pleasure from putting someone else first. It has to work both ways, though. You know the cliché about give-and-take." She thought about it. Her answer was a cliché in itself. The pat answer, the textbook answer that had nothing to do with reality. Maggie was just looking at her. She had probably spoken like a stuffy old maid teaching Marriage 101. But being married didn't necessarily mean that she knew a lot about marriage. "I told you it was complicated," she said.

As easily as she had slid into seriousness, Maggie left it. "All the more reason for me to avoid the subject," she said. "Have another cup? I'll fix this one."

They stayed for another twenty minutes or so, until Maggie got a call. It was obvious that the caller was a man, and Leah took the opportunity to wave goodnight and slip out. She figured that whoever he was, he related somehow to the conversation she and Maggie had just had.

The night was still and frosty, and Leah could see her breath in the cold air. She unlocked the door of her car, which was parked under a large streetlight, got in, and locked it back. Marriage. She ought to have something to say on the subject. Maybe it had been too long since she had given much thought to marriage, in general, and hers, in particular. Where was her's headed? What did it mean to her anyway? Good questions. They were too complicated, just as she had told Maggie. Perhaps she would have to come to terms with some of those questions, eventually. Yes, of course she would. She and Clay couldn't perch on the cliff forever. But not tonight. It made her weary to think of it tonight.

She turned on the ignition, the heater, and the radio. A string version of "Have Yourself a Merry Little Christmas" oozed around her. Christmas was everywhere. But it didn't bother her in the car. If she could keep from going home, just keep driving, she could listen to Christmas songs all night.

Pulling out into the street, Leah sang with the violins. The words came easily, without thinking about them. She was thinking of Maggie on the telephone, trying to picture the man on the other end of the line.

At school, all the children seemed to walk a couple of inches off the ground. "Settle down!" Leah ordered, again and again, although she had known since the first of December that the command had lost what little effect it had carried in the beginning.

Edward was perhaps the only one who did settle down, and then, not in the way Leah had in mind. While the other children flitted about the room on the pretense of significant business, Edward slouched in his chair, his eyes fixed somewhere above their heads, or, more likely, he folded his arms on his desk and bent over, face down. He had lapsed into periods of indifference plenty of times before, but always, his refusal to participate was clearly rooted in defiance. Now, that didn't seem to be the case. He wasn't causing trouble or setting himself up as an example before the class—*See, I don't have to do anything I don't want to do.* There was a shift in attitude here that Leah couldn't quite put her finger on.

She began to wonder if perhaps Edward wasn't well. Back in November, he had missed a whole week with the flu, and now it occurred to Leah that he hadn't had much color in his cheeks since. Maybe he was anemic. She felt sure that he, like most of the other children from this area of the city, received nourishment mainly from sweets and salty snacks.

She asked him several times if he felt all right, and he always responded with a nod. That was about as far as she was ever able to delve into the matter. Usually the noise level heightened whenever she focused her attention on one child, and she had to turn to the class and say, "Settle *down*, students!"

Mr. Carlton stopped in one afternoon, and as it happened, he couldn't have chosen a better time. A soft roar hung in the room, to be sure, but the students were busy on an art project, so the noise and disorder were excusable. Edward, at that particular time, had gone to the rest room. Mr. Carlton nodded approval as his eyes made a sweep of the four walls. Leah's Christmas bulletin boards had been decorated just the day before, but maybe Mr. Carlton didn't realize that.

"Looks like a nice activity," he said, examining Danny Blount's wire sculpture. "What kind of wire is this?"

"It's what florists use," Leah explained. "I wanted something that was green and also very flexible." She didn't bother to say that she'd had it on hand for a couple of Christmases now.

"Good job," Mr. Carlton told Danny, who grinned with his whole face.

"Yes, this is nice," Leah said. Danny had just about finished his wreath, complete with ribbons and bells.

She got the feeling that Mr. Carlton might have lingered at the door—maybe he had come by to say something in particular— but a group of girls charged out of the rest room, a few doors away, and their laughter rang through the halls, so he left, hurriedly, just as Edward meandered into the room.

There was something comforting in knowing that this wasn't an easy time of the year for any of the other teachers, either. Confusion rippled throughout the school, as special activities superseded the routine. Each grade was allowed to take a field trip at Christmas time. This year, the fourth grade went to the new Performing Arts Center to see *A Christmas Carol*, done especially for children. For a three-hour field trip, there was a week's worth of flurry, before and after. It was the same for the Christmas program that the Conroe Chorus was preparing. On the last day of school before the holidays, the program would last for thirty minutes at best, but Emily, Teresa, Corey, and Danny popped in and out of class a couple of times each day, as they were called to special practices.

Leah utilized every minute of her planning period. There were always papers to mark, materials to sort out and put away, and when those chores were done, she made calls in the teachers' lounge. It was the first time she'd used the Yellow Pages to do her Christmas shopping, but she found that it did save a lot of legwork, as she checked with various stores to see if they had what she needed. Some stores even delivered. But even if she had to make a stop after work, she could hurry in and out. No browsing this year.

During her planning time, there were usually no other teachers in the lounge, which was fine with Leah. In the mornings, since all the talk had turned to family gatherings, holiday preparations, and children, Leah rarely came to the lounge. Not that she deliberately avoided it, actually, but she was getting to school later these days. There was so much to get done, at home as well as at school. Wrapping packages to mail turned out to be a bigger job than she remembered from years past. She wound up making several stops at the post office, and there were always lines. Packages headed for Denver got a late start, but she sent them airmail and called her mother that night to say that the presents were on their way.

Leah remembered what Clay had said about staying busy, and she decided that he had been right about that much. But there was busy, meaning *keeping occupied*, and there was busy, meaning *being pressured for time*. It was the latter that Leah understood now. When you busied yourself with petty tasks, just for the sake of staying occupied, time lagged and you still thought too much. But when you were genuinely rushed, your mind was absorbed with each duty at hand. And during this holiday season, Leah was rushed.

More than anything, her job at Maggie's Rags was her salvation. It took the chunk from each day that had potential for reminiscing too much. And, beyond that, it was fascinating. Every day Leah met women whose lives glittered, and men, too. Men who spoke to her with admiration in their voices, not compassion. She could step out of herself for a while at Maggie's shop. And so, December was not the monster of a month that she had feared. It was not a joyful month, either. There were times when all the laughter and anticipation crowded in on her like bad air. She thought about the grinch who stole Christmas, the Dr. Seuss character who tried to keep Christmas from happening for anyone because it wasn't happening for him. Well, she knew how he felt. The grinch was the villain, and maybe she was a grinch, but she would write Christmas off the calendar if she could.

That was exactly what she was thinking one afternoon when the director of the Conroe Chorus brought some notes around about the program. Edward was up at the front of the room, tossing some paper in the trash can, and Leah asked him to pass out the announcements. "These notes should be taken home to your parents," she explained to the class. "They tell about the program that the school chorus is performing on the twentieth. Parents are invited. Teresa, Danny, Emily, and Corey are the chorus members from our room. I'm sure their parents will be here, and all parents are welcome."

She noticed that Edward had delegated his responsibility to Corey, who was zealous about the job of distributing the notes, and who made sure that each student put the paper in a safe place. Edward was back in his seat, scooted down on the end of his spine. Leah had learned to watch for the signals, the lull before the storm. She called Edward up to her desk.

"What happened?" she asked.

"Nothin'."

"Didn't you want to pass out the notes?"

He shook his head, looking away. Leah considered again how pale he was.

"Are you sick, Edward?"

"No," he said, firmly.

"Well, what is it then? You seem. . . . " She started to say *sad* but changed it. "You seem quiet."

A spark came into his eyes, but he spoke with an edge that was more like disgust than anger. "I hate Christmas."

Leah let the words settle, and then she asked, "Why is that, Edward?"

"I just do. I'll be glad when all the fuss is over."

Another grinch, Leah thought. Maybe there were a lot of their kind running around. Kids so poor that they knew better than to even wish. Adults who, for whatever reason, knew that Christmas would not measure up to what it was supposed to be.

She said, "You know something? Sometimes I feel the same way. I'll be glad when all the fuss is over, too."

She smiled at him, and for the first time that she could remember, Edward managed to smile back.

11

Clay wasn't so busy. During the first part of December, he spent a lot of class time in review, which cut down on his work outside of class, as well. Preparing exams was his biggest task, and next to that, tying up some loose ends for the curriculum committee so they could shelve their work until the first of the year. Once exams were taken, there was a rush to compute grades, but that was over quickly. As Clay looked toward the holidays, the three-and-a-half-week break stretched out before him like the Grand Canyon.

He had not seen Carmen Kennedy for weeks, but he had thought of her. Once, walking across campus, he had a glimpse of a girl in front of him who could've been Carmen. There was something in the way she tossed her head and the way the sunlight struck her hair that kept Clay from looking away. He knew, after just an instant, that she wasn't Carmen. Her hair wasn't exactly the right shade, and the girl lacked Carmen's brisk, confident stride. But he watched her until she took a different direction from him, and he kept thinking that she *could* turn around, and he *could* be wrong.

Another time, he heard Carmen on the radio. He was driving home from Arden one evening as dusk settled on the brown fields along the highway, and he heard her. She was making a commercial for the Community Players' current offering, *The Gift of the Magi*. "A story of love," she said, in the rich voice that Clay knew well, even though she never gave her name. For several days after that, he listened for her. Each time he was in the car, he tuned in to the same station and listened, and each time he arrived at his destination feeling a little cheated.

The last day of office hours was warm and sunny. It was strange, Clay thought, as he stood at the window of his office and watched people without coats going about their business. Strange that tomorrow was the start of Christmas break, and today, a group of guys were tossing a Frisbee in shorts and T-shirts. Even the girls in sweaters were more in keeping with October than mid-December. Where were the snow flurries, the gray, boiling skies? How could anyone muster up Christmas spirit in this balmy weather?

Most of the students who were still around were loading cars, and it looked a lot like the exodus at the spring break. Clay had a good view of three parking lots. Not as scenic as the quad, which could be viewed from the other side of the building, but there was always activity. Over in the student parking lot, two girls were trying to close the trunk of a car. They slammed it, and it flew back up. They slammed it again and leaned on it, but obviously, it wasn't fastened. They raised it again, and Clay could see all the junk, piled high, that hampered their efforts. The girls talked, gesturing a lot, and one left. *Probably to get some rope*, Clay thought. He shook his head and grinned. He had a good mind to go out and offer his assistance, advise them to rearrange their cargo, or, better still, ditch half of it. But maybe someone else was having fun watching them. Why spoil the show?

Then he saw Carmen. As he looked back to one of the faculty lots, she was crossing, coming toward his building. He had no doubt about where she was headed. What he did doubt was whether it was a good thing. For a minute he thought he'd leave, duck out the exit at the end of the building or withdraw to the men's room for a few minutes. But he didn't. He waited at the window, his back to the door, and he found himself jingling his change, impatiently, before he finally heard her voice.

"Hello, Dr. Padgett."

Most visitors leaned around the door and waited to be invited in, but Carmen came straight over to the window and stood within a polite distance of Clay.

"Come in, Carmen," he said. "Don't be shy."

"Did I do something wrong? Already?" Her grin was shaded by an I-don't-quite-understand look. *I know the joke's on me, and I don't mind, but why?*

Which made Clay feel a little like a bully. "Forget it," he said, trying to erase it with his hand. "It was a bad joke. Would you like to sit down?" He indicated the chair in front of his desk and started to his own chair.

"No, thanks. That's where your students sit and chew their nails while you lean back and say, 'Uh huh, uh huh.' No, I'll stand."

"I'll be glad to rearrange the seating if it'll make you more comfortable," said Clay.

"Thanks, but I really don't have time to get comfortable, and I don't want to take much of your time, either."

"I'm not that busy."

"Funny. I always get the feeling that you are." Something in her voice lifted then, and she said, "Hey, I didn't come to make war. I don't know what it is about us, but we always seem to be jabbing at each other. Why is that, I wonder?"

Clay didn't know how to answer. Maybe Carmen wanted him to say, *Because we intimidate each other,* but he wasn't going to. Before he found any words, however, Carmen went on. She pulled an envelope from her purse and tossed it on his desk. "Here. I came on a peaceful mission, to deliver tickets to our play. We're doing an adaptation of O. Henry's *The Gift of the Magi*. Everyone says it's wonderful." Then she added, "Maybe you and Leah would like to come." She watched him as she said it, and Clay could feel all the questions that were inherent in that one sentence.

"Thanks," he said. "I wish we could. You keep offering us tickets, and I keep having to decline, but I promise, someday we're going to take in one of your plays."

"You came once," she reminded him.

"That doesn't count. Maybe in the spring."

She nodded, but *Yeah, sure* was what came across, and Clay felt compelled to keep the records straight. "Leah's working evenings and weekends at a dress shop, and she's still teaching, too, so she's putting in long hours. But it's only through Christmas, and then I think she'll enjoy getting back into the mainstream again. Seeing plays, eating out, all those things that she hasn't been interested in since T. J.'s death. Working at Maggie's Rags has given her a real boost."

"Maggie's Rags? That's where she's working?"

Clay nodded. "You know the shop?"

"Yes, I've bought clothes there a couple of times. It's a fashionable place. I can't afford it very often."

"Neither can Leah, but she does like her job. She's caught up in it." He picked up the envelope and toyed with it, running his thumb around the corners.

"So. What does that mean for you?"

Carmen's eyes were so intense that Clay had the feeling she was right at him instead of four feet away and separated by his desk. She did have a way of intimidating him. It was true. Yet, he had the urge to tell all, and then, on the other hand, he had the feeling that she knew it all already. "You really want to know, don't you?" he said.

"Yes, I do."

Clay was vulnerable, and knew it. What he was needing and had needed was to know that someone considered *his* well-being, for a change. Somehow that had been lost in concern for Leah, and for their marriage. Well, he was a person in himself, too. That was what was so messy about the whole situation with Carmen. He was vulnerable, and she was available. She cared, and made no apologies for it.

"If you won't sit down," he said, "let's go outside. Did you drive or walk?"

"I walked."

"Then I'll walk back with you. This weather's too nice to waste."

"Fine, if you're not afraid to be seen with me."

"The campus is a public area. I think I'm safe."

The browns and grays of the campus looked enough like winter, but today the air retained only a mild nip, more like a hint that winter is coming. Early on, Clay shed his coat and slung it over his shoulder. He fixed his gaze some few feet in front of him and found it very pleasant walking, very easy talking.

He told Carmen how Leah had been at first, after T. J. had died, and how she was finding her way back, slowly; one step forward, one step back, sometimes two steps forward. That was the way it had been, and the backward steps were always disappointing, because even though you expected them, you could never prepare yourself. Now since Leah had started working at Maggie's Rags, she was enjoying people again, and she seemed happier than she'd been in months. As for himself, what could he do but try to support her and hope that when the work at Maggie's ended, whatever happened wouldn't be too devastating?

Carmen was a good listener, Clay thought. The entertainer that she was, she knew when *not* to make wisecracks, too. She hardly commented at all, except to speak some sort of affirmation whenever he paused. But when he had finished with a question, she said, "You can't do anything but support her, Clay. You're the kind of person who couldn't live with yourself unless you gave your marriage every chance."

"Thanks for saying that," he told her.

"Thanks for telling me where you are," she said. "I haven't been coy myself, but, considering the circumstances, I'll behave if you think we can be friends."

"I'd like to be friends," he said.

"Good. Then I'll bring you some more tickets sometime." She laughed softly. "This turned out to be a good idea, didn't it?"

"What do you mean?"

She flipped her hair, spreading it out on her shoulders, all shimmery in the sun. "Well, last summer I gave you some tickets. Believe it or not, I didn't have any ulterior motives. I just knew you liked the theater and I wanted you to see the Community Players. But we sort of got off to a nice start. Then maybe I pushed too hard. Anyway, I didn't like being at outs with you. So I thought, *Why not go back to square one?* So here we are at square one. Maybe I won't make the same mistakes, and maybe we can actually be friends."

Clay said, "You need to learn that when you manipulate people, you don't tell them that they've been manipulated."

"I just wanted you to know my intentions were honorable," she said. "Now you can trust me."

At the door of the dramatic arts building, Clay said, "I left those tickets on my desk. I meant to give them back to you."

"It's not necessary," Carmen told him. "Pass them on to someone who appreciates sentimentality at its finest."

"That doesn't sound exactly complimentary to the play. Didn't you say it was wonderful?"

"Oh, our people do a marvelous job with the story, and the public seems to crave melodrama at Christmas time. But you'll have to admit, the self-sacrifice bit is a trifle overrated."

Clay started to say that he didn't find it so at all, but why end a pleasant conversation on a sour note? He said, "I gave the other tickets to some friends who would probably enjoy this play, too." He was thinking of Ben and Catherine.

"Fine. Or, who knows? Maybe you and Leah can work the play into her schedule." Tossing her head, she said, "It would probably be a good one for her to see."

Walking back, Clay thought of what Carmen had said about knowing where he stood. He was glad they had cleared the air, and he was glad she wasn't pushing. She had said he should give his marriage every chance, hadn't she? Well, he was. He hadn't broken any rules. He had done nothing more than unload a little misery on a friend. That was all, he told himself, trying to shove aside the inkling that in some strange way he had let Leah down.

While school was in session, Clay had spent only evenings and Saturdays alone. Now, during Christmas break, being alone had become the norm. Most days, since Leah, too, was out of school, she went to the shop at noon and worked till nine. Sometimes Clay wished he had never heard of Maggie's Rags, but there was another point to consider. How would he and Leah spend their time if they were both at home during Christmas vacation? A good question, since they didn't seem to have much to say to each other now, not even enough to fill the few hours that Leah was home in the mornings.

Reading, which had always been a pleasure, if not a near obsession, lost its appeal after a few days. Six hours a day with a book could sustain even an avid reader just so long. Clay took up jogging again, getting out in the late afternoon to establish a routine that he could keep up when he started back to work. But you didn't jog five miles, right off. You had to start in small doses. For now, the whole procedure of changing clothes, jogging his limit, and showering took about thirty minutes.

On a few occasions, Ben and Catherine invited Clay over for dinner, and he accepted. Those were pleasant evenings. Their house was Christmasy, and Ben and Catherine were so comfortable to be with that Leah's absence didn't matter too much. But coming home on those evenings, Clay was more aware than ever of how hollow his own house was. It lacked not only the warmth of Christmas, but warmth in general, a sense of being no more than a dry shelter.

Agnes, the cleaning woman, for all that she lacked on other accounts, was perceptive enough on that point. "I seldom ever find a house like this," she said to Clay when she made her weekly call, on a morning when Leah had gone to work at nine. Agnes had made one round through the house, winding up in the garage, where Clay was finally making a place in the corner for the lawn mower. She was still wearing her black coat, a version, Clay guessed, that was new in the fifties, twenty years before Agnes received it from someone she worked for. She was small and birdlike, and now, as she turned to lecturing, she even sounded a little like a scolding magpie. "I don't see as how you need a day's work from me when there's nothing to do but a little laundry. Oh, I'll run the vacuum all right and go over the furniture, but me, I like to look back at the end of the day and say, 'Now don't that look a lot better?' As far as I can tell, this whole house looks just like I left it last week. It don't even look like anybody's living here!"

It was the feeling that Clay had, too, that he and Leah kept certain hours at this place, but that the substance of their lives was being lived out elsewhere.

Agnes put in the day, but not without frequent complaints. After she had dusted in T. J.'s room, she interrupted Clay's lunch to tell him her opinion of rooms that were kept "for the departed." "As long as you keep everything in that room the way it was, you'll never give him up. Take it from one who lost a husband and two children—a son in Vietnam, and long before that, a dear little girl, just turned two, struck down with pneumonia." This she said in a kinder voice. "And let me tell you how hard it was to take down that baby bed. But still, life has to go on. The best thing you could do would be open up that room, change it up, make it a sunroom or a study for you— seeing how you have a lot of books all over the house—and I guarantee you, it'll do you and Mrs. Padgett a world of good." Then as an afterthought, perhaps just to cover all the bases, she said, "I wouldn't tell you any different, either, if I'd known your little boy."

On her way out, she remarked, "Not much time left to get your tree up. Most folks already have theirs done. I've been sweeping up pine needles all week." And then, a final word, half-whispered around the door: "If you could just get a little Christmas into the house, it would count for a lot!"

Clay watched her march up the sidewalk toward the bus stop, chin out, shoulders back. As dogmatic as she was, Clay really hadn't minded her company too much. And he had to admit that she made a certain amount of sense.

The Sunday before Christmas was damp and dreary, typical of December in Tennessee. But the weather was all that was typical this year, Clay thought, as he started a fire in the fireplace, and he said to Leah, "This is sort of a funny holiday season for us, isn't it?"

"Funny? I hadn't thought of it that way," Leah said.

"Funny as in strange."

Clay was wadding Friday's newspaper, and he had come across an announcement that the *Messiah* was being performed that afternoon. "We've missed a lot of Christmas activities that we usually attend. The Christmas parade, the *Messiah,* things like that. Remember, last year we went to the *Nutcracker?*"

"I remember," said Leah. "We had to walk two blocks in icy rain. My shoes were ruined, and I caught a terrible cold."

Clay added a couple of sticks of wood. The fire was catching up, the kindling crackling. He could build a good fire. That was something he'd always taken pride in, even though it was a little thing—the one-match fire. Your logs had to be placed just so, and you didn't need a lot of kindling, but it had to be dry. The arrangement of it was the key, letting enough air through, but not too much. Some people never got the hang of it, and it was usually because of the air principle. Ben Anderson, for one, had told him he'd never managed a one-match fire, and Clay had enjoyed showing him how easy it was. He liked things that you could count on if you used the right formula. There weren't many things in life like that. There weren't many formulas, when you came right down to it.

Clay stood with his back to the flames and clasped his hands behind him. The fire wasn't drawing to the point of giving out heat yet, but there was something in the motion of backing up to a fireplace that gave the illusion of warmth. "We haven't been Christmas shopping together this year," Clay said. "I've always enjoyed that, taking a night and making the rounds at one of the shopping centers. That's the one time of year that I like to shop. I've missed that."

"There was just no time for it this year," said Leah. "But I've managed to do my shopping in bits and pieces. This is my last gift, if I haven't forgotten anyone. It's for Catherine and Ben."

Clay came over to inspect the needlepoint that she was doing. The part of the cloth that she was working on was some sort of flower basket.

"When did you get time to do this?" he asked.

"Oh, I started it in the summer," she said. "I bought the kit when I didn't have anything to do. I ordered it from a little catalog. It took me hours just to fill out the order blank." She stopped and watched the flames in the fireplace. Clay wondered what memory she was nurturing. But she turned back to her work all at once, and her voice was cheery. "There's really not too much to it. The kit even includes the frame. I remembered it a few days ago and decided to finish it for Catherine and Ben, since we're going to their house Christmas evening." She spread the fabric out on her lap. The pattern was a flower garden scene in shades of purple. "Do you think it's all right?"

"I think it's fine. They'll like it."

"Well, since they invited us over for Christmas," she said again, and then looked up at him. "I wonder why they did that."

"I don't know what you mean."

"I just thought it was strange, that's all. Why would they want to spend Christmas evening with us?"

"Because they don't have any family here, and neither do we. It sounded like a perfectly logical idea to me."

Leah took up her stitching again. When she didn't say

anything, Clay added, "We've been friends with the Andersons for a long time."

"Yes," Leah said, "but Catherine is jealous of my friendship with Maggie."

It wasn't like Leah to make that sort of rash statement. Clay looked closely at her face, trying to see her eyes, but Leah kept looking down at her stitching, running the needle in and out with a steady, easy rhythm.

"That wouldn't be like Catherine," he said, baiting her.

"Maybe I'm being a little unfair, but I have had that impression." She sounded more like Leah now. Clay wondered if he would always be watching, listening, holding his breath for that extra second whenever Leah appeared to be a fraction off-target. It was such a habit now. "Oh, Catherine is a good friend, all right," Leah went on, "but there's a strain with us now. I can't put my finger on it."

Clay backed up to the fire again. "Has she said something about your job at Maggie's?"

"The usual bit about my working too hard. You can't please some people. I never thought Catherine was that way, but I'm beginning to wonder."

"Don't be so hard on her. She's always been there for you."

"Maybe I don't need her so much any more," Leah said, meeting Clay's stare. "I don't need her pity."

"You're imagining things," Clay said, with more of a snap than he'd intended.

"Now I'm suffering delusions. I'm paranoid, right?" She stood up and tossed the needlepoint into the chair. "Clay, won't you *ever* let me get well?"

She left the room before Clay could get any words together, before he could even get a grip on what the last minute was all about.

Clay was the first to awake on Christmas morning. For a couple of hours, he had wavered on the border between sleep and wakefulness, but something heavy had pushed at him, refusing to let him cross over. Finally at nine twenty, the sun slid through the crack between the draperies and reached in with long fingers, tugging at his eyelids. He sat up quickly, swinging his legs off the bed, wondering why he'd tried so hard to sleep, anyway. Sure, it was Christmas, but you couldn't blank out a whole day, sleeping. The memories wouldn't go away, all the memories of T. J. stampeding to the Christmas tree to find his loot. You just had to wade through them, that was all.

"Wake up." He leaned over and shook Leah's arm. She twisted a little but didn't open her eyes. He wanted to say, *Well, let's get on with it*. Last night hadn't been the most joyous Christmas Eve he could remember, but he hadn't complained about Leah working. If work was what she needed at that particular time—and obviously it was—well, that was all right. But he was determined to have a little support this morning. "Come on. It's 9:30. Get up."

Leah barely opened her eyes. "What's wrong?"

"Nothing. It's just time to get up."

"What's *wrong*?" she asked again.

Clay realized that he did sound angry—perturbed, at least. Something churned inside him, something restless and, yes, maybe angry, too. But he hadn't intended to lash out at Leah. He took a deep breath and leaned back on his pillow, his hands folded behind his head. "I'm sorry. I guess it annoyed me when I realized I'd overslept."

"Overslept? Clay, it's a holiday. We don't have any schedules to keep this morning. You can sleep as long as you want."

No, I can't, he thought, but he said, "Well, I'm ready to get up. How about you?"

"I guess so." She still didn't move.

Clay looked at the swirls in the ceiling, squinting a little. Swirls in plaster were sort of like clouds. You could make almost anything out of them. The profile of a girl with ringlets, a cake topped high with frosting, a dragon, a train.

"I guess we need to get to the Andersons about four-thirty," he said.

"Probably."

"Do you have any plans for the rest of the day?"

"Not really. I bought a ham to bake this morning. We can have ham and biscuits later."

"Fine." He sat up again, and this time he got to his feet and dressed quickly. Leah had hardly changed positions. "Come on," he said. "Get up."

"I am. I am." She scowled at Clay and sounded a little impatient, but she dragged herself out of bed.

"I'll make coffee and pour us some cereal," Clay said.

"Whatever."

He went to the kitchen and started the coffee. Then he went into the living room and plugged in the lights on the small, artificial tree that he had put up himself last week—for Agnes, perhaps. There were two gifts under the tree now. Good for Leah. He went through the records under the stereo and found his favorite Christmas album. It was a collection of carols sung by some little-known choir of eighty voices. The album had been a free gift when they bought their stereo, some eight or nine years ago, but more than any other record they owned, this one, those eighty voices, captured Christmas for him. At least it always had, and he was counting on it today. He set the album in place, ready to drop on the turntable at the flip of the switch.

Leah was in the kitchen. Clay heard her rattling dishes, and he saw that she was getting out bowls. "I thought you were fixing us some cereal," she said.

"I will."

"Never mind. I'll do it."

They both ate hurriedly, for some reason, or at least it seemed so to Clay. When they had cleared the table, he said, "Come into the living room. I have something for you."

Leah followed him. She glanced at the twinkling lights and said, "Did I tell you I like the tree? Thanks for putting it up. I just didn't have time."

"I know." He reached for the smaller present and handed it to her. "Merry Christmas."

She opened the package too carefully, Clay thought. Most people would shake a small box like this to hear if it rattled first. No, he was being too picky. *Forget it*, he told himself, as Leah drew out a gold chain embellished with a small diamond. But still, he'd like to see a little more energy in this ceremony.

"It's beautiful," said Leah. She unfastened the necklace and slipped the two ends around her neck, backing up to Clay. She held her hair up. As Clay fastened the chain, he thought about the birthmark at her hairline, a tiny red splotch that made an almost perfect heart. Leah had never worn her hair up because of the mark, but Clay had always told her it was attractive, and now it seemed even more fascinating as a few dark strands of new hair made wisps around it.

Leah ran her fingers around the chain and touched the stone. "I need a mirror," she said, "but go on and open your gift first. And thank you." Perhaps she realized how empty the words sounded, because she kept trying. "I love it. Really, it's beautiful."

"It looks nice on you," said Clay, and it occurred to him that his words were just as empty. Even when he unwrapped an overcoat, the kind he had wanted for two seasons, he wasn't able to put any more substance into his thanks than Leah had. "It's just what I need," he said, trying it on, "and it fits well, as far as I can tell. I guess I need a mirror, too."

Leah said, "Last night Maggie's friend from New York came to pick her up from work, and he was wearing an overcoat just like this one. Exactly. Even the same shade of tan. He's a banker named Alan Rush. That's about all Maggie has told me about him, but I gather that they're very close, since he's spending Christmas here."

"Must be." Clay didn't care about Maggie's friend, and he certainly didn't want to hear about him now. He turned to the stereo and switched on the record that had always sent Christmas rushing upon him in great waves.

"What are you doing?" asked Leah.

"I thought a little Christmas music would be nice."

"I still haven't framed the needlepoint for Catherine and Ben," said Leah. "I need to wash my hair, too." She gathered up the torn paper, taking care with the bows, which she saved from year to year. "First I guess I'll put on the ham. It'll take a couple of hours."

She left the room, as eighty voices broke into a jubilant chorus of "Angels We Have Heard on High." It was rousing, just as Clay had remembered, but somehow he wasn't surprised that the Christmas spirit, whatever that was, failed to descend on him. He got comfortable in one of the chairs and listened to the rest of the album, six carols in all. He was still wearing his overcoat.

Maybe he would check the antifreeze in the cars today. Maybe he would see what he could do to the front door that had been sticking since they put in new carpet last winter. And it was only a few hours until they could head for the Andersons' house. He could look forward to that. It would be nice to celebrate Christmas with people who didn't have any problems.

12

"I always like beginnings," said Maggie. "Especially the beginning of a new year. I never put much stock in New Year's resolutions, but I do get the feeling every year that I'm starting over, starting with a clean slate. You know what I mean?"

It was Saturday, time to open the shop. Leah unlocked the door for business, but she was glad that for the moment no customers were in sight. "Yes, I know what you mean." She had said the same about school, that each August was a chance to start fresh. Even this past year, with all her apprehensions about going back to the classroom, she'd had some of that feeling.

"That was what I liked most about college," Maggie said. "Each semester was like an entire book, with a beginning, when every class had a new feel to it, a middle, when you could get comfortable in a routine, and an end, when you tied up everything. Then you closed the book and took a break."

Leah smiled. "That's one way to put it." She was checking the sale rack to make sure all the clothes on it were marked down. Sure enough, one Nippon suede didn't belong there. Probably Becky had hung it on the wrong rack last night. "We're not marking this down, are we?" she asked, holding it in front of her.

"No, none of the Nippons. Check the whole rack, will you?"

Leah shuffled through the hangers of clothes and held out the sleeve of a charcoal wool. "Now this one is supposed to be on sale, but it's not marked down." She came up to the counter and punched on a calculator. Then she went to the rack again with a red pen and changed the price on the tag. "Becky should be more careful."

"I think I'll have to take the blame for that one," said Maggie. "I did the markdowns."

Leah kept from looking straight at her by checking a few more price tags. "Well, everyone slips up now and then," she said.

Maggie laughed. "Don't misunderstand. I'm glad you're so observant, and that you take such an interest. I'd like to keep you."

Leah did glance at her then. She wondered if Maggie was just being polite, but she couldn't tell because Maggie had turned her attention to an inventory sheet. It could be a hint, Leah thought, but no, the arrangement had been, from the first, that she'd work through Christmas holidays, and that meant that today was her last day. Monday she'd go back to school full time, and the sales would be over, for the most part, and Maggie would be in good shape with the college girls she'd employed before. Even if Leah were asked to stay on, she wondered if she could. The weeks before school dismissed for Christmas had been a strain, for sure. Physically, not mentally. She'd been in good spirits all along, better than she'd anticipated. But could she keep up the pace indefinitely? Probably not. Then there was Clay. She had told him that her job here was temporary, just through the Christmas holidays, and he'd never said much, but she knew he hadn't been 100 percent for it. He would have plenty to say if she told him she wanted to keep working at Maggie's. He'd say she wasn't being fair to him, and maybe that was the truth.

She went to another rack to check sizes. There wasn't much point in worrying about what Clay would say because Maggie wasn't going to ask her to stay on anyway. Easy solution. Everybody ought to be happy with it. She wished she were.

"Kind of slow this morning, especially for a sale day." Maggie leaned across the counter.

"Uh huh." Leah had the red pen between her teeth as she

sorted through the size ten suits. She pulled out a wool tweed with a pleated skirt and inspected it.

"Something wrong?" asked Maggie.

Leah took the pen from her mouth. "I could have sold this twice if it weren't such a strange color. We don't have a blouse in the store that blends."

"The color is celery." Maggie came out from behind the counter and began checking blouses. She held up a silk print in shades that Leah would call army green and olive. "This is supposed to go with that suit, but you're right. It doesn't do much for it."

"I tried white, but the combination is blah."

Maggie returned the blouse to the rack, and took a long, scrutinizing look at Leah. With her hand on the curve of her hip, she gave a mocking scowl. "You didn't get much of a rest over Christmas, did you?"

"A rest? No, not really. Why?"

"You're a little edgy this morning. That's why. I'm a terrible slave driver, Leah. You should've just said, 'Whoa, Maggie, I'm putting in too many hours.'"

"Oh, it's not that at all, Maggie," Leah said. She was embarrassed now. This was her last day, and everything had been fine, all along; straight A's. Until she had come in complaining today, blowing it all. "I guess I *have* been a grouch this morning, haven't I?"

"You're probably just tired. I get the same way when I'm overworked. I let the smallest things annoy me, like clothes hanging on the wrong rack." She cut her eyes at Leah and grinned.

"Well, maybe I am tired," said Leah, "but I want you to know, I never would've managed to get through Christmas if I hadn't had this job. I mean it. I think I would've landed on the funny farm." Not to mention what would've happened to my marriage, she thought, if she and Clay had spent all that time together. But she didn't say it, of course, and she didn't have to explain why

Christmas was difficult. Maggie knew just enough about Leah's personal life to accept Leah's silence on those subjects that were off limits. That unspoken agreement was one reason that Leah was so comfortable with her.

"It worked out for both of us," Maggie said. "When Rosemary left, I was in a panic. I tried to tell myself, 'Maggie, every time you depend on somebody else, you get hurt, in one way or the other. It doesn't pay to count on anyone but yourself. You'll manage alone. You always have.' But still, I couldn't see my way through December without going crazy. Then you happened along, and what did I do? I started depending on you, just the way I depended on Rosemary. I guess I'll never learn."

She laughed, and Leah knew that she didn't want to be taken too seriously, even though she was quite serious. Leah didn't know exactly what to say, but before she could decide, Maggie took up another subject anyway. "You never told me how Clay liked his overcoat."

"Oh, he liked it." She reached around her neck and found the gold chain. "I don't think I've shown you my present from him, either."

Maggie took the diamond in her fingers and examined it. "What a lovely gift. So thoughtful. I imagined that all wives who didn't get clothes for Christmas got toasters and waffle irons. This ought to restore my faith in the institution of marriage."

Leah thought about Alan Rush, the man who had come from New York to spend Christmas with Maggie. "You haven't mentioned any of your presents. Anything special from New York?"

"Yes, as a matter of fact, a tapestry for my living room. Alan collects art objects as a sort of hobby." She took a deep breath. "And then there was this other gift that I had to refuse. That sort of put a damper on the holiday. But he should've asked first, before he spent his money. I mean, I've known Alan for four years, and he ought to know by now how independent I am."

"Are you talking about a ring, Maggie, the engagement kind?"

"That's what Alan was talking about. It was a gorgeous diamond. But that's not why you say yes. Right?"

"Right. But don't ask me *why* anyone ever says yes, because I'm not sure. I can't remember that far back."

Maggie gave her another hard look and then she broke into a laugh. "I'll miss you, Leah. You don't really want to stop working here, do you?"

"No, I don't."

Maggie stopped laughing. "You don't?"

"No."

"Then why are you quitting?"

"Because you only hired me through the Christmas holidays."

"I don't believe this! You had enough confidence to ask me for the job in the first place, so why didn't you tell me you'd like to stay on?"

"I didn't think you'd need extra help after the holidays."

"Well, you were wrong."

Leah felt silly, like a schoolgirl answering to the teacher for a foolish mistake. Like chubby little Angela who threw up on the cafeteria floor earlier in the year. Leah asked later why she hadn't told her she needed to leave the cafeteria. Angela had answered sheepishly, "We're not supposed to leave the cafeteria during lunch."

Leah said, "If you can use me on Saturdays, I'd like to stay on."

"I can use you." Maggie's confident smile, the slight nod of her head were as good as saying, "That's that." She moved back behind the counter with the grace and ease that never left her for a minute, so it seemed, and Leah had to admit that Maggie could and would have managed alone if it had come to that. Maggie would never break her stride over a matter like this, a matter which Leah, in contrast, saw as a hurdle.

Thinking of another hurdle, she said, just as the first customer appeared, "Let me check out my plans with Clay tonight, just to be sure. Do you mind?"

"Of course not." The bell on the door made a cheery tinkling sound, and Maggie turned her smile on Mrs. Gardner.

Mrs. Gardner, glamorous for fiftish, swept inside. "Good morning, Maggie. There you are, Leah! I was hoping you would be here today." Then to Maggie again: "Julie *raved* over the outfits that Leah talked me into getting her for Christmas. So I wanted to buy another one for her to take back to college. She leaves tomorrow, you know. I was hoping Leah could help me, since she made such a hit with the others."

Maggie smiled graciously. "I'm sure she can."

When Leah spoke to Clay about working Saturdays, his response was, "Whatever you want to do, Leah. Whatever will make you happy."

When she thought about it, it was exactly the reaction she should've expected. Hadn't he said something similar when she told him, weeks ago, that she'd taken the job at Maggie's? He had said it was her decision, more or less, but that wasn't the same as supporting her in it. Now, she was careful to say that she hadn't actually given Maggie a definite answer, that she wanted Clay's opinion, but he was taking the same easy out. Maybe that was his defense: *If you crack up under the pressure, if this breaks up our marriage, you have only yourself to blame. It wasn't my choice.*

"I'm not really surprised about this," Clay said. "I could've predicted that you'd want to go on working there. So, in a sense, I've already accepted it. You ask what I think. Well, I think this conversation is just a formality."

Always so rational, so even-keyed, in a way, he was like Maggie. They were both survivors, self-possessed, with a kind of ho-hum way of looking at the world. But that composure was attractive in Maggie. It didn't wear so well on Clay, though Leah couldn't say exactly why.

"If you object, Clay, if you think my working Saturdays will somehow make a problem, I wish you'd say so."

"I wouldn't try to keep you from doing something that's so important to you. I guess when we come right down to it, you *need* the job."

"Does that bother you?"

Maybe I've picked the wrong time for this discussion, Leah thought. Clay had just come in from jogging, and she'd detained him on his way to the shower. He sat on the edge of the bed, his face shiny with perspiration, giving inordinate attention to his feet. His running shoes might have been lead, for all the effort he exerted to pull them off, making a grimace and a little groan with each one. Even with his socks, he made a production of crossing each leg and peeling off the sock the way you'd peel a banana. Now he was preoccupied with the dead skin on the ball of his right foot.

"Does it bother me that the job means a lot to you? No, I'm glad something does."

"You're being a child, Clay!"

Now she got his attention. He looked up at her, but his voice was still cool and even. "I don't know what you want from me. My blessing? Well, I gave it. I can't believe you want to be talked out of this, but maybe you just rehearsed all your arguments and you're disappointed that I didn't give you a chance to use them. I don't know. I'm tired of trying to figure it all out, Leah. I'm tired, period." He stood abruptly and pulled his shirt off over his head in one swift motion.

"You've been big on talking things out," said Leah, sounding peevish, even to herself, but she didn't care. "So if this is going to be a problem, let's *talk* about it."

Clay's voice was not unkind. "We have so many problems, Leah, that this one doesn't seem to amount to a grain of sand," he said. "I'm going to take a shower."

New beginnings, Leah thought, as the children arrived in new clothes, showing off new playthings. Teresa had stiff new jeans, embroidered on the pocket. Emily wore a new ski jacket. Some of the boys had new jeans and shirts, too, but boys didn't say much about clothes. They talked about sports equipment and remote-control race cars. Corey had brought his electronic basketball game, and the boys gathered around, taking turns with it. Leah wasn't surprised that Edward was absent, this first day back. If you didn't have something to show or brag about after Christmas, it would be hard to face your fourth-grade peers.

But Edward showed up on Tuesday. He was one of the first to arrive, and he ducked into the room almost before Leah recognized him.

"Edward?" She caught him with a gentle hand on his shoulder. "Is that you?"

He turned his face up toward her and made a little sideways grin. He was a different child, in appearance, anyway. His greasy tangles had surrendered to a fresh haircut and a thorough scrubbing. "I like it!" Leah said. What she liked particularly was the clean shine, but the cut was stylish, too, not a shaved look, which was so often the result of a trip to the barber shop.

She could see that she was embarrassing him, the way he cut his eyes toward the floor, so she simply added, "We missed you yesterday."

"We went to my grandmother's in West Tennessee and the car broke down so we didn't get back." It was the most information that Edward had volunteered all year.

"Thank you for telling me," she said, nodding him away, noticing that his hands and fingernails were clean, another first. And as he walked across the room his new tennis shoes squeaked on the wood floor. Leah was puzzled by the West Tennessee expedition. She wondered if that had been the reason for these changes. Maybe his mother had decided she'd better clean him up before they visited his grandmother. Or maybe the grandmother took more interest in him than his mother, and she was the one who bought the tennis shoes. *He could've used a coat,* Leah thought, as she watched him dig into the pocket of his jacket, torn at the shoulder seam. *But this was, at least, a beginning.*

She kept watching him, and she felt her mouth try to fly open when he pulled out an electronic game. Why had she thought he wouldn't have anything to show for Christmas? She'd taught in this neighborhood long enough to know that kids who did without proper clothes weren't necessarily the ones who did without toys. It was all a matter of priorities. Still, with Edward, she was surprised. He'd never been like some of the others, pockets full of candy each morning, and every Monday, a handful of cheap trinkets from a discount store. It had something to do with the West Tennessee trip, she guessed.

"Hey, you've got football!" Corey said to Edward. "That's what I really wanted, but I got basketball instead. You wanta swap?" He held out the game that he'd brought again today.

"Naw!" said Edward.

"I don't mean for *good*. I mean just for a minute."

Edward hesitated. Then he said, "For a minute," and handed his over, taking Corey's.

Danny and Buddy were in the room now, and they joined the two other boys.

New beginnings, Leah thought. She hoped so.

Edward had not come to school early since before cold weather, but one sparkling sunny morning he was on the steps waiting when Leah arrived. This time a smaller boy sat beside him, both hunched over, holding their shabby jackets around them. When Leah greeted them, Edward mumbled, but the other child peeped, "Good morning!" and grinned, showing two missing teeth.

"And who are you?" Leah asked.

"His brother." The little boy swung his thumb toward Edward.

He did resemble Edward when you thought about it, Leah decided. Their hair was the same, in color and cut, and their faces were shaped alike, oval, with high cheekbones. A pretty shape, though

Edward would fight if you told him so. But the smaller boy was a more animated version, without Edward's pout and dull eyes.

"Do you go to school here?" Leah asked.

"No ma'am."

"He's just five," Edward put in, and, oddly enough, he sounded exactly like a big brother.

"Oh. You don't go to kindergarten?"

"I didn't have my birthday in time. I'll go next year." He grinned again.

"What's your name?"

"Wendell."

"I see you've lost some teeth, Wendell."

"I got 'em knocked out a long time ago. You wanta hear about it?"

There was something so spontaneous about the child, so refreshing, that Leah laughed. "I'd like to hear more about *you*," she told him. "What are you doing here?"

Wendell made an exaggerated shrug. "I don't know. I just walked to school with him."

"Will you walk home by yourself?"

"Go on," Edward said to his brother, all at once.

"Naw!" Wendell sprung back, scowling. "Not till school starts!"

"Go on, now!" Edward nudged him.

Wendell's face fell, and then he shrugged again, to Leah. "I just go up the street, up to Miz Dortch's."

Now Edward took hold of his arm. "I'll take you to the sidewalk, and you'd better go on, like I said!"

It was all very strange to Leah, why Edward was so annoyed at his brother, why he was getting rid of him, but then, she'd never understood Edward's reasoning, anyway. Still she wondered, *Who is Mrs. Dortch? A baby-sitter?* She guessed Edward's mother worked, but she was sure he wouldn't tell her where.

"Be careful, Wendell," Leah said. "And I'll see you in a few minutes, Edward."

Wendell made a half turn and said, "See you later!" but Edward pulled him back around, muttering—scolding him, probably—as they went away.

Leah had always said that January was the month when most learning took place, unless there were snow days. This year the first snow held off for the whole month. And there was a period that found the children fresh, settled, intense about their studies. It was part of the gearing down after the Christmas hype. With no big holidays in sight, they anticipated any break in the routine, a special science project, a filmstrip, a math game. But even in day-to-day tasks, the students took the business of school more seriously than they had all year. Leah hoped they were learning.

Then, after an interval of mild, almost springlike days, the snow came. It began one morning as rain, and by that night the skies had dumped six inches. Schools dismissed early, but the streets were already treacherous and tangled with traffic. "A regular snowstorm," the deejay said as Leah left the school parking lot. "And everybody has the same idea—get home early. The interstates look like big crawly caterpillars. So take it easy, folks, slow and easy. Get ready for a long drive home."

An hour later, when Leah unlocked her kitchen door, the phone was ringing. "I'm glad you made it without any trouble," Clay said.

"I took the back roads instead of the interstate," she told him. "The radio says the interstates are terrible."

"I'm just starting home."

"I thought you might cancel your last class."

"The administration frowns on that," he said. "We're like mailmen. Neither rain, sleet, nor snow—you know. Anyway, I'll be leaving in a few minutes. I have no idea how long it'll take."

"Just be careful," said Leah.

"I will."

Leah went through her afternoon routine, picking up a

banana in the kitchen, switching on the radio in the bedroom, changing into jeans and a sweater. "Nashvillians don't get enough practice to be good drivers in snow," the deejay said. "We've got a mess throughout the city. Fender-benders, stalled cars, and bumper-to-bumper traffic on every main artery out of town. If you don't have to get out, folks, stay in!"

Leah wondered if the snow had let up at all. It hadn't, she saw, holding back a fold of the curtain. In one yard, two boys without hats or boots threw snowballs at each other. A girl, wrapped in snow gear befitting an Eskimo, pulled a sled through the white street. A dog ran circles around her, kicking up a spray of snowdust behind him. Everyone loves a first snow.

Leah left the window and turned up the heat. The house, all at once, was as cold as a tomb.

Clay had come from his last class in a hurry, like his students, and now he realized that he'd left his fountain pen on his desk in the classroom. It would probably be there tomorrow, he told himself, but on the other hand, a silver electroplated fountain pen was a little more tempting than a fifty-nine cent ball point, so he'd better not take the chance.

The classroom on the second floor looked out over the quad. Clay lingered at the window a moment, tucking away his pen. Snow made the campus a fantasy world, a storybook picture. At the far end of the quad, a dozen or more students were into a heavy snowball fight. Most classes were over for the day. They seemed to have adjourned to the outdoors. So much activity, so much laughter; the students played in groups or in couples. Snow had a way of bringing out the child in everyone. Clay saw a couple passing below on what was the sidewalk, though you saw only ruts and tracks. They were laughing, of course. Everyone was laughing. The boy scooped up a handful of snow and dumped it down the girl's back. She made a snowball and aimed as he ran, but before she could let it go, her target's feet slipped out from under him and he toppled into the snow. She ran toward him, hitting the same slick spot, landing beside him. Clay left them trying to bury each other.

He was already set to leave the building, briefcase in hand, but he went back to his office instead. He looked up a number in the faculty directory and dialed.

Carmen answered.

"Carmen, this is Clay. How do you like the snow?" He tried to sound light, matter-of-fact.

"Why, I love it, of course," she said.

"I expected to see you outside in one of those snowball fights."

"If it weren't that teachers have this stuffy image to maintain. . . ." Carmen laughed. Then she stopped, at once, and said, "You've never called me before. Not here."

It was true. He had seen her, talked with her, several times during the past few weeks, but always their meetings had been by chance. Perhaps. How could he say for sure? They often saw each other at lunch, but what brought them to the student center or the faculty room on the same day, at the same hour? Still, calling her was something else. He said, "I remembered how you used to drive in snow. You were awful. Are you any better now?"

"Probably worse," she said. "It's funny you should think about that. I was thinking about college, too, about that winter when we went to Gatlinburg so much. Do you remember the time you sprained your ankle?"

"I remember." He hesitated, but even the pause, he thought, said too much. "If you need chains on your tires, there's a filling station just two blocks away where you can get them. They'll do a good job. I bought some there last year. I assume you don't have any chains."

"You assume correctly. You know me, never prepared. I assume you *do* have chains."

"Well, yes, I've carried some in the trunk all winter. I guess I ought to put them on before I start back. You don't have as far to drive, but still, it wouldn't be a bad idea to go by that service station. It's on the corner of University and Sixteenth."

Carmen's voice was softer now. "Thanks, Clay. But someone offered to take me home and give me a ride in the morning. I was glad to get out of driving, so I guess I'll just leave the car here."

He was quick to say, "That's good. Sure. That's the thing to do. I'm glad you've got a ride." *Male or female?* he wondered.

"Thanks for calling anyway. I'm surprised. I mean, it was a *nice* surprise."

"I just happened to think what a bad driver you were in snow." He tried to laugh, but suddenly he felt so foolish, so transparent, that he cut off the conversation as quickly as he could. "Take it easy," he said.

"Enjoy the snow," said Carmen.

The drive to Nashville took almost two hours, and each mile Clay told himself what a blunder he'd made. The next time he saw Carmen, she'd either laugh at him for being such a schoolboy, or she'd make the move that naturally followed his. Either way, he'd taken a step too far. No, too close.

Catherine called the next morning. "Did I wake you up?" she asked.

"No," said Leah, "but you would have ten minutes ago. It's nice to have a day off from school."

"We'll probably be out tomorrow, too, unless the sun really works today," Catherine said. "I'll never get used to Nashville snows. They paralyze the city. In North Dakota, as long as we could shovel snow away from the doors and get them open, we'd have school."

"This is much nicer."

"I agree. But North Dakota's still in my blood. I like to get out on days like this. So I was wondering, if I drive, would you like to go somewhere for lunch? It would be such a treat to have lunch somewhere besides the school cafeteria."

Leah saw, from the kitchen window, a whole gang of neighborhood children out in the street behind her house; children, sleds, snowmen. "Yes," she said, "that sounds fine."

"Good! I'll be there at eleven-thirty. Be thinking about where you'd like to eat. I'll drive anywhere you say."

They had lunch at a tearoom at Palmer's Square, not far from Maggie's Rags.

"This is wonderful," said Catherine when they'd finished. "I'm glad you knew about this little place."

"I've been here a few times on Saturdays," Leah told her, "but most of the time I don't go out. Saturdays are busy days at the shop, and besides, Maggie has all kinds of snacks in the back, the office, I guess you'd say. Cheeses, nuts, crackers, fruit, exotic teas. Snack is really too ordinary a word. Maggie is certainly no ordinary person, and she doesn't do anything in the ordinary way."

"Mrs. Blake, at school, seems very personable, but I've never dealt with her very much." Catherine glanced at her check.

Leah saw no real connection between Maggie and her mother—not in this conversation—but of course Catherine didn't know Maggie. Maybe she *had* gone on a little too much, Leah thought. She said, "Mrs. Blake was very kind when we talked about Edward Curtis."

Now she'd struck a chord. "How *is* Edward?" Catherine could always get interested in school. Leah wasn't *dis*interested in school, but the hours she spent at Maggie's Rags were so much more colorful. She, herself, was a more colorful person at the shop than at school. But it was doubtful that Catherine could understand that.

"Edward's still a mystery. He came back from Christmas, scrubbed, with a haircut and new shoes, after a trip to his grandmother's. Now he's as grimy and slouchy as he was before. But he's working some, and he doesn't get into as much trouble now. He and I have a better rapport. That's something."

"That's a lot."

"I guess so."

"Have you ever met his mother?"

"No, I think she works. I doubt that she'll show up at the next parent conferences, either. But I've really given up on getting any help from her."

Catherine mused for a moment. Then she said, "Maybe she's just not aware of all the problems, since you never have made contact with her."

"She *must* be aware of the problems," Leah snapped back. "She can see that his clothes are shabby, that he's dirty, and I'm talking about *layers* of dirt, too. Maybe they're poor, but housing projects do have water. There's no excuse for a child coming to school filthy."

She had raised her voice, and Catherine didn't argue. They paid for their lunches and went out into the brisk air. The sun was working, all right, only to make slush that would ice over tonight when the temperatures fell again. There was little chance of school tomorrow.

"Is there anywhere else you'd like to go?" Catherine asked, turning on the ignition.

"I can't think of anywhere." She used to have a good time with Catherine, but it was different now. She wasn't sure exactly why.

Maybe Catherine was thinking, too, about how it used to be, the all-day shopping expeditions or the movie matinees, because she said, "We ought to get out like this more often. Of course, we don't have many days off from school. And now you're busy on Saturdays." When Leah didn't reply, she went on. "But I'm glad you enjoy your job at Maggie's Rags. I'm glad you and Maggie have become friends. I think she's been good for you."

Catherine sounded sincere, but her kindness—if that's what it was—grated on Leah. Catherine had always been a mother hen. She wouldn't change. But Leah had heard enough about what was good for her.

"Maggie isn't always telling me that I ought to get on with my life," Leah said. Maybe she'd intended for her words to sting, because that was how they came out.

"People who tell you that *care* about you," Catherine said. Catherine, the long-suffering one. "They—*we*, I should say—could help if you'd let us."

"How could you help, Catherine? You keep saying it, but how? I know you mean well, but it's so easy for you to say, 'Get on with your life, Leah,' without the foggiest notion of how it feels, knowing you'll never hold your child again." She let out a great sigh. She was as shocked as Catherine was at the words she had spoken. There was a cold pause before she said, "I know you mean well."

"But you're right," said Catherine, staring straight ahead at the road. "I've never had a baby to hold in my arms, so I couldn't know how to miss that, could I?"

It had been behind Catherine's smile all along, Leah knew now, but she hadn't seen it. Now that she saw it, what could she do? She could say she was sorry, but words were flimsy. The truth was, she could do no more than Catherine could do for her, which was nothing.

13

It was the month for snow. After the first big one, the salt trucks got their systems down, the school buses traveled alternate routes that bypassed troublesome hills and icy bridges, and drivers began to get the hang of functioning in snow. It was reassuring, Clay thought, to note how adaptable the city was.

Dirty white patches still lay along the sides of streets, but traffic to the Vanderbilt games was as heavy as ever. Clay had asked Reverend Kent, on his way out of church Sunday, if he liked basketball. "I'm crazy about basketball," the pastor had told him. Clay had said maybe they could go to the game on Thursday night, that he'd call him and try to work it out. He hadn't expected the arrangements to be so easy. Carson Lewis came into his office the next morning with two tickets for sale, and when Clay called, Reverend Kent's calendar was free.

Inside the gym, Reverend Kent said, "I haven't been to a game since last year. This is a treat, Clay."

"Glad you could make it. I've been to a couple this year, but I enjoy it more when I'm not by myself." He hoped Reverend Kent wouldn't ask about Leah just now, although he realized that he'd unintentionally made an opening. "How about some popcorn before we find our seats?" he said.

"Sounds good."

They edged toward the concession stand and bunched with a crowd who'd had the same idea. Clay got a glimpse of George Kirby's hair just as Reverend Kent said, "Is that Bruce McSwiney, up there getting a hot dog? And the young man beside him has been coming to church, too. His name is George Kirby."

"George was in one of my classes last quarter," said Clay.

"Is that so? Were you responsible for getting him to come to our church?"

"Maybe the first time. But Ben Anderson has taken George under his wing, I think, and I couldn't be happier about it. I like George, but he's the kind who needs a dose of reassurance every time you see him. I'll confess, I couldn't help getting impatient with him when he was in my class, even though he was a top-notch student. But Ben has a way of making a person like George believe in himself."

"Ben's good at that, all right."

Bruce saw them first, and he and George made their way toward them. Bruce hadn't been in the college and career class when Clay had worked with that group, and George and Reverend Kent only knew each other from shaking hands at the door of the church, so the four spent a moment getting acquainted all around. Then Clay said, "George, it's good to see you again." And he meant it. He hadn't talked with George since last quarter, and he found himself wanting to hear that everything was all right with him. Bruce and Reverend Kent moved out of the path to the concession stand, and Clay and George stepped aside, but in a little different direction.

"I've been wondering how you came out on your grades," said Clay.

"I kept my scholarship by the skin of my teeth." George was fidgety. Even as he held his popcorn and soft drink, he seemed to need something to do with his hands. "I got off to a good start this quarter, but now I'm in trouble again. I don't even have any math courses. Can you believe it? A math major taking botany and bowling? I had to have a dumb PE class. If I ever get through these required courses, I'll do all right. Math's the only thing I care about."

Clay wished he could tell George that the curriculum committee was recommending some changes in course requirements for scholarship students, more options in class selection. Basically, their recommendations, if taken, would give the best students the better breaks. But by the time the administration made a decision, George's future would already be decided.

"You're right," said Clay. "If you can hang in there through this year, you'll have it made."

"It doesn't make sense," George said, swishing the ice in his cup. "Why can't students get into their major without first having to wade through three quarters of murk?"

"Every student isn't as enthusiastic about his major as you are, George. Some need exposure in a lot of fields."

"But for those of us who know what we want to do it's ridiculous."

Old times, Clay thought. He didn't disagree with George, but he was feeling a rise of impatience. He wondered if Ben was ever annoyed with George.

"I've been seeing you at church," Clay said.

"Yeah, I've been a few times."

Bruce and Reverend Kent joined them again, and it was just as well. Clay wondered why George got under his skin. Maybe because he understood the young man so well.

After a few minutes more, Bruce said, "We don't want to miss the starting lineup."

"Bruce goes to Vandy," George said. "We've got seats on the second row in the student section."

"Right in front of the cheerleaders," Bruce pointed out.

"Have a good time," said Clay. "We'd better get our popcorn."

"Nice kids," Reverend Kent said when they were gone.

"Yes, they are." In spite of George, Clay felt good about him. At least, he'd found a friend.

The crowd carried the thrill of a home win out of the gymnasium, and Reverend Kent was as vocal as any of the other animated fans in the stream that poured through the exits.

"That last shot was something, wasn't it? What pressure! One point behind and two seconds on the clock. He hadn't been making his shots tonight, either. But that last one was the one that counted. What a beauty! Never touched the backboard."

Clay liked basketball, but winning or losing, he couldn't say he ever got carried away. He had to grin, remembering how Reverend Kent had jumped up out of his seat and joined all the yelling during the last ten seconds. "It was a good game," Clay said.

"It was a great game!"

The crowd branched into several tributaries, still moving swiftly. Clay had left his car on a side street, and it was a good hike to the parking place. Others ducked their heads and leaned forward into the cold, but Clay saw no point in rushing. There was no fast way to get out of the Vandy area on a basketball night, anyway. Better to let the traffic thin out than to fight it.

"You said you liked basketball. Now I believe it," he said.

Reverend Kent laughed. "I hope I didn't embarrass you."

"Not at all. I was glad to see you enjoying yourself."

"I wish I had time to see more games. That's something I just don't get around to doing. But I do love basketball. I played in college, myself, a long, long time ago." He stressed the last words and laughed again.

"Somehow that doesn't surprise me," said Clay.

Now they were away from the lights around the gym. Clay watched his breath crystallize in the air in front of him, and he saw that the stars were out, blinking in the cold sky. A car door slammed here and there, but the noises and the voices all seemed far away. Clay fell into a slower stride.

"Tell me something." Reverend Kent slowed down to match Clay's pace. "Was there some other reason that you asked me to the game tonight, such as, maybe you had something on your mind?"

Clay dug his hands deep into his pockets. "Does it show that much, or are you just very perceptive?"

"Maybe a little of both." He waited a half dozen steps or so and asked, "Is it Leah?"

"It's Leah, and it's me, too." The words were hard to get out, and he hesitated before he said the rest. "As perceptive as you are, you've probably guessed that we haven't had much of a marriage since T. J. died. I don't know whether we have a future together or not." He felt a rush of relief, having said it. No matter how Reverend Kent responded, Clay was glad that finally he'd given some shape to the anxiety that kept gnawing at his insides.

Reverend Kent asked, "What does Leah say about it?"

"Nothing. We don't talk," Clay said. "I used to try, but now I'm not even sure I want to. I told you it wasn't just Leah. Not anymore."

Reverend Kent didn't say anything for a moment. Then he asked, "What can I do?"

It was an unexpected question, and Clay contrived a half-hearted laugh. "Maybe I thought you'd give me a good swift kick."

"Or at least put up an argument?" Reverend Kent looked at him for the first time and grinned.

"That's right. Tell me how wrong I am to feel such miserable self-pity. Tell me how I ought to keep holding on, and that in time Leah will come around. Maybe I just need someone to scold me and remind me of my responsibilities."

"You've always taken your responsibilities seriously, haven't you, Clay?"

"Yes. Sometimes I think too seriously."

"Then you don't need any words from me on that. As for what you feel—self-pity or anger or whatever—I wouldn't presume to tell you that your feelings are wrong. I'm sure you've learned, somewhere along your educational pilgrimage, that feelings aren't right or wrong. They just *are*."

"I've always believed that one should, and could, maintain a level of control," Clay said.

"Control of actions, yes. Of feelings," he paused, "one can deny what one feels, even to oneself, *mostly* to oneself, I'd say, but I'm not sure one has much control." His voice rose to a warmer, kinder note. "But we're speaking theoretically now. You wanted to talk about you and Leah."

Did he? Clay wondered what there was to say, really. Reverend Kent was a good sounding board, though, for whatever nonsense came to mind.

"It's strange how tragedy draws some couples together, and separates others," Clay said. He couldn't seem to keep from talking in generalities.

"You're saying the trouble between you and Leah all stems from T. J.'s death."

"Of course!" Clay heard his answer come out more sharply than he'd intended.

They were at the car now, and as Clay unlocked the doors, Reverend Kent said, "I have to ask you this." They got inside, and perhaps he thought he hadn't been heard, because he said again, "I have to ask you, Clay. Is there another woman?"

Again, it was a question that caught Clay cold. He fumbled with his keys. The engine turned and a cloud of vapor rose from the exhaust. The car behind had already moved, and Clay backed a few yards before making an easy maneuver out into the street.

"I have never been unfaithful to Leah," he said.

He had not seen Carmen Kennedy in three weeks, since before the first snow. Feelings—all right, he wouldn't deny that there were some unsettling feelings where Carmen was concerned, but he had never for a moment forgotten his commitment to Leah. Carmen had nothing to do with the state of his marriage.

Reverend Kent settled back in his seat, crossing his arms, looking thoughtful. "I've counseled a lot of couples who have been through tragedies together. Some marriages tend to become stronger, but I'd venture to say a great many more fall apart."

That's a real consolation, Clay thought, but he kept quiet.

"I wonder why it is that married couples have such difficulty comforting each other, at the times when they need comforting most."

Clay said, "Maybe it's because grief is such a personal thing. You can't do someone else's grieving, even if that person is your spouse."

"But it's natural to turn to *someone*."

He felt Reverend Kent's eyes on him as he said, "There's no one else."

"Then maybe there's still a good chance for you and Leah." Reverend Kent believed him, Clay was sure, almost sure. "You have good instincts, Clay. Trust yourself."

Clay could not tell him how afraid he was that he would, indeed, trust his feelings. Nor could he tell him just what that would mean. "Let's just stick to basketball," he said. "What kind of game is Vandy going to give U.T. next week?"

The last meeting of the curriculum committee stretched on until dusk.

Clay loosened his tie as he walked over to the only window in the conference room where they met. "This was a long one," he said. "A long, tedious one."

"We would've stayed until midnight to keep from having another meeting," Shirley Nettleton said, gathering all the files of rough drafts into her arms, as the person with the task of getting the report printed. "I think we've all been looking toward the end for weeks."

"Yes, I know." He laced his fingers behind his neck and stretched until his knuckles popped. "I just keep thinking that we've probably left something undone. Something important."

"I'm sure we haven't," she said. "But if we have, someone after us will take care of it. There's only so much that a human being can do. Or five human beings. I think we've done a remarkable job, and I don't mind saying so." Her heels clicked on her way to the door. "Do you need any help closing up?"

"There's nothing to do but flip off the lights. I've got to get my stuff together first."

"Take my advice and get away from here," she said.

Clay turned around and gave her a quick smile. "Don't get blown away out there. I just saw Carson chasing his hat."

"As long as the wind's warm, I won't complain. Incidentally, I plan for this report to come out in time for us to celebrate the vernal equinox. I've set that deadline for the printer."

Clay said, "And if he knows what's good for him, he'll meet it."

"Good-night," said Shirley. "Go home."

It was kite weather, for sure. The warm wind was a little on the gusty side, and some of the novices out on the baseball field would no doubt get their strings snapped by a strong puff, but dozens of enthusiasts had managed to get their kites out. It was some sort of fraternity-sorority contest. Clay didn't know the particulars. He had just seen all the kites as he left the faculty dining room, and he'd meandered over to the field, lured by the fluent, rhythmic dance of the bright shapes against the blue sky.

This was the first week of the year that had promised spring. Nothing had come to life yet, but the sunshine was splendid, and the wind smelled clean, new air that had pushed winter away. The mood of the campus was optimism. Clay wondered if he was the only one at the university who didn't share the euphoria. He had noted the subtle currents in his classes, and here on the baseball field, there was nothing subtle in the display of high spirits. Girls giggled, clapped, jumped up and down, and flirted with the guys. Guys laughed, pointed, yelled to the kite fliers, and kidded around with the girls. Around the edge of the field was a thick ring of spectators that included some teachers, as well as students. Clay wasn't surprised that Carmen was among them. Maybe he had known she'd be there. This was the kind of event that would attract Carmen. And the baseball field was just across the street from the dramatic arts building. Maybe that had occurred to him, too. Still, he told himself that he had come for the kites, and he raised his eyes toward the moving colors in the sky. When he looked back to where Carmen had been, she was gone.

I have to ask you this, Clay. Is there another woman?

I have never been unfaithful to Leah.

It's natural to turn to someone.

There's no one.

A moan rose up from the crowd as one of the kites broke off and took its own course. Like a bird given freedom, it soared up and away, and finally out of sight. A few of the kites were hardly more than specks. The contest was quickly narrowing down to those who knew what they were doing. It might be a drawn-out procedure from here on, and Clay had classes.

He moved away from the crowd, scanning it once more from a distance. Then he turned and crossed the street. Halfway across, he saw Carmen coming down the steps of the building. She waved. He waved back. She stopped at the bottom step, and Clay knew that for whatever reason, she was waiting for him. And, for whatever reason, he was glad.

"I saw you earlier, watching the kites," he said as soon as he was close enough not to shout. "I guess you have just as good a view from here." He took a quick glance over his shoulder, but the kites were so high now that from this vantage point you couldn't tell much about them.

"I saw you, too." She sounded a little breathless. "Then I came back to my office for this. I was hoping I wouldn't miss you." She handed him an envelope with Arden Community Players printed on the front.

Clay took it and said, "I think I halfway promised, didn't I? What's the play this time?"

"It's a little musical you may have heard of. *Camelot*. And guess who's playing Guinevere?"

Clay tapped the envelope against his palm. He knew what she was doing. The first time he had seen Carmen Kennedy was at the opening of an amphitheater in Gatlinburg, and she was Guinevere, in flowing white, lovelier than even Lerner and Loewe could have imagined Guinevere to be.

"You've had plenty of practice, I guess."

"High school, college, and once at a little regional theater near L.A., besides that summer in Gatlinburg. Yes, I know Guinevere inside out. It's always so exhilirating when she runs away with Lancelot."

She was still on the first step, which put her on his eye level. He wondered if she'd planned that. Her eyes were like cat's eyes, green and bright and clever. They searched his face and read every thought, he was sure. There was a strategy at work here, and Clay, for all his logic, felt himself being drawn into whatever whirlpool Carmen was preparing for him.

"I haven't talked with you in a while," he said.

"I've been avoiding you." Her lips turned into a grin, and then she took it back. Without a flicker of reservation, she said, "You needed time and distance from me. Don't ever let it be said that Carmen Kennedy doesn't have a sense of fair play. If your marriage was working, I would know that and respect it. It was working when I came back from L.A., and I left you alone. But when I saw you out there today, I could tell that you were no better off than when I was confusing you. I could just tell, because I know you, Clay."

"For the record," he said, "you've never confused me more than right now."

Carmen tried to brush her hair out of her face, but the wind had it in wild tangles. She gave a quick smile, pushing back golden wisps that kept blowing into her mouth, and she said, "I can make it simple for you. There's one ticket in that envelope. Just one. It's a pass for opening night, and that's next Friday. I want you to be there."

Carmen had always been able to shake him up, but this time Clay couldn't even make a witty comeback. All he could say seemed to come from somewhere in his subconscious: "I'm not ready to give up on my marriage."

"It's not that I don't feel sympathy for Leah," Carmen said. "Losing a child was a horrible thing, and I'm sorry she had to suffer. But losing you was her own fault."

No, she hasn't lost me, he thought, but he couldn't say it. As he labored for words, a couple of girls came out of the building, and in the inverval while they passed, Clay tried to sift through what was going on. This moment was inevitable, but he had denied that it would ever happen. He was a reasonable man, and yet, he had duped himself—not Carmen, but himself—by the pretense that nothing between them would come into accounting. Hadn't he known? Of course. He had known all along.

"I haven't been fair to you," he said.

"You never made any promises, so you never broke any. You've said all the right and proper words, but I expected that. I told you. I *know* you. I understood that you had to give your marriage every chance. Well, you have."

"I can't give up on my marriage yet." More right and proper words, but he said them with more conviction than before.

Carmen looked at him with an arrogance that was as frightening as it was fascinating. "I'm not asking you to give up anything. Just come to opening night. I'll look for you. Just be there, Clay. It doesn't have to mean anything that you don't want it to mean."

But it would, he knew. If he showed up, it would mean something. It would mean everything. And he knew that she knew it, too.

Leah's car was not in the garage when Clay came home, and the house was dark. In the kitchen, a note was stuck to the refrigerator door with a magnetic ladybug. Clay knew when he saw the scribbling that it was written in a rush.

"Clay, I promised to meet Maggie at the airport. She's been to

N.Y. on a buying trip. Plane arrives at 6:40. I called your office but you were in class. Sorry I forgot to tell you earlier. You can warm up tuna casserole (thawing on top of stove). I don't now how long this will take. Leah."

"You picked the perfect evening for it," he said out loud. His voice had a hollow ring to it. He wondered how she'd like it if he called her at the airport, had her paged. But what would he tell her? *Come home and fight for me, Leah. This may be your last chance.* Wouldn't that be the icing on the cake? He wadded the paper into a tight ball. Wouldn't it, though?

14

The night before the statewide teachers' meeting, Leah checked the alarm setting on Clay's clock. "I need to get up when you do," she said. "Did I mention that the teachers' meeting is being held at Jackson State this year?"

"No, but I heard it on the news," he said. He had wondered if she'd get around to telling him about it.

"We don't have to be there until 8:30, but I'm not used to driving that far, either, so I'm giving myself plenty of time."

"It's not a bad drive."

"But you drive it every day. I'm not sure where to park."

"It's not a big school, and you have, at least, been there before, though not very many times."

"No, I haven't had the opportunity to visit very often." Leah scowled at him. "What's *with* you, anyway?"

"Nothing." He had been sharp, but not for any reason that he could explain to Leah.

"I thought I might try to have lunch with you, if you were interested," she said.

"Fine. Can you wait till twelve-thirty?"

"We're supposed to have lunch at eleven-thirty. That's the only time we aren't scheduled for meetings."

"I have a class at that time."

"I guess lunch is off then."

"I'm sorry." Clay switched off the light. The open window brought in the smell of night and growing things, and Clay felt like going for a walk, but it would be too much of a hassle to explain.

"Are the meetings just tomorrow, or Saturday, too?" he asked.

"Just tomorrow. There's a banquet tomorrow night, but I didn't care about going."

Clay kicked the covers down to the foot of the bed and twisted and turned until he finally got comfortable on his stomach. "Good-night," he said, talking into the pillow, muffling the words.

"Good-night."

Tomorrow was Friday. And tomorrow night was not only the occasion of a banquet to culminate the teachers' meeting. Friday night was opening night for *Camelot* at the Arden Community Theater, and Clay still had his pass.

Leah had chosen a session on positive classroom management with Edward in mind, but the room was chilly and the seats were hard. In less than ten minutes, she had decided that the speaker had credentials, but no secrets, and her mind started taking side trips.

She remembered how Maggie Blake had looked, entering the holding room at the airport last week. Of all the female passengers who had arrived from New York, Maggie was the only one who looked the part. Some of the men in business suits could have come straight from Wall Street, but the women, even the ones in executive attire, were drab beside Maggie. It was something more than Maggie's linen suit, her leather purse and matching shoes, her shopping bag from Sak's that gave her style. It was the sweep of her walk, the angle at which she held her head. When Maggie entered a room, it was hers.

And the strangest thing was, when Maggie had sought out Leah and they were standing there together, Leah had felt admiring eyes on both of them. She didn't feel slouchy beside Maggie, not at all. She felt as beautiful, as confident, as Maggie seemed to feel all the time.

"You're a jewel," Maggie said. "I'll buy you dinner for your trip out here. Unless Clay's expecting you at home."

"No, he's not." For an instant there was a twinge of what? guilt? regret? But she told herself that Clay was no happier in her presence than in her absence. Maybe she was just wishing she'd left him something besides a frozen tuna casserole.

It turned out to be a cheery evening, and Maggie sprinkled dinner with wonderful descriptions of New York. Leah wondered how it would be to make the buying trip with Maggie, or for her. For the first time, she could see herself leaving the classroom behind, with no qualms at all.

Rosemary was not coming back to work. Leah had been in the shop on Saturday when Rosemary called and talked at length with Maggie. Her baby was six weeks old, and perhaps it was because she'd had such an "iffy" pregnancy that she was so very happy with her healthy boy. She wanted to stay at home for a while, indefinitely, maybe until he started to school.

"Some women are just made for mothering," Maggie had said when she hung up, "and some for nurturing careers. I'm sure now that I misread Rosemary's calling. But she was so competent! Tell me, Leah, where will I find a replacement?"

Leah and the other part-timers had helped to hold things together during Rosemary's leave, but now Maggie was actively looking for another assistant. If she found one, Leah would probably have to go. She realized that. On the other hand, if *she* offered to take over that capacity, Maggie would snap her up in a minute. She was sure of that, too.

Leah tuned back in as the speaker said, "The child who is bored will find something in the classroom to interest him, and he won't bother to ask whether it's acceptable to the teacher and the rest of the class."

How many times had she heard the same cop-out? If a child was disruptive, he was probably bored, and that was the teacher's fault. Teachers were blamed for everything. If a child slept through class, it had to be that the class failed to challenge him. It couldn't possibly be due to the fact that his parents let him stay up till midnight the night before. And if a child didn't pass his test, it was because the teacher hadn't made the content interesting. When you had an Emily Harper in your class, no one ever gave you credit for anything she knew. She was just unusually bright. She had come there precocious. But Leah knew who was blamed—albeit, silently—for Edward's behavior, even though he had come to her hostile.

Maybe she was burned out.

She couldn't do much for Edward, anyway, this late in the year.

Maggie's shop was like a playhouse, of sorts. Working there was hardly work. It was playing dress up.

What did she owe to her profession, anyway?

What would Clay say if she just quit?

It was the last session of the afternoon. If she left now, she could probably catch Clay at his office before he started home. She slipped out of her seat, which was, fortunately, only four rows from the back, and eased out the door. She would just ask Clay, or tell him. Whatever.

As one who considered himself proficient at inductive and deductive reasoning, Clay figured he ought to have more resources at hand than he was able to summon, and it annoyed him. It scared him, too. He could talk in theories, but when it came to figuring out the solutions that were actually significant, his inclination was simply to ditch logic and go with his feelings. Wasn't that what Reverend Kent had told him to do, anyway? So, if that was the route he'd decided on, the next question had to be, What did he want to do? And there he was stumped.

Clay leaned back in his swivel chair, propped his feet up on his desk, and read the writing on the blue pass: *Entitles bearer to access backstage.* Carmen meant business. Why did that surprise him? He had known, even in school, that she went after what she wanted and usually got it. The only reason she didn't get him then, he remembered, was that she wasn't sure she wanted him. Of course, that was all before Leah. When he had met

Leah, whatever he'd felt for Carmen quickly turned to fog.

But Carmen was right about at least one thing: his marriage wasn't working, and it hadn't worked for a long time. Would it ever? Leah, at this point, seemed content enough to live in the kind of time lapse that had characterized the last few months, the last year, actually. Well, he couldn't be happy with that anymore. He had to have some reason to go on trying. That part didn't have anything to do with Carmen.

But what did he want?

He held the question up like a prism, turning it in the light to see every side, every angle, but the images that reflected on the walls were all distorted. He closed his eyes and tried to convince himself that he was making too much of the whole thing, that there was no reason to make any decision—today—about the direction his life would take. But that was no good, either. He had told Carmen he'd been unfair to her. He had been unfair to Leah, too. Worst of all, he had been unfair to himself, but today he would get it straight, one way or the other.

You have good instincts, Clay. Trust yourself.

What did he want?

When Leah leaned around the door, Clay jerked, and his chair would have turned over backwards if he hadn't been close enough to the wall to brace himself.

Leah laughed at him and closed the door behind her. "I caught you," she said, "although I don't know what I caught you doing."

His laugh, he noticed, sounded a little nervous, but Leah didn't seem to be put off. "I'm innocent. You just startled me." He laid the blue pass face down on his desk and straightened up. "I don't see you at my door very often."

"This will keep you on your toes."

Leah's smile was easy, relaxed. She was very pretty today, and not in a remote way, as Clay sometimes saw her beauty. She had on a khaki-colored suit and a blouse in purplish-reds that tied at the neck. It was an outfit he remembered from last year, maybe a couple of years ago, but he didn't remember that it had ever looked so right. The perfect teacher look.

"How was the teachers' meeting?" He got up and began to gather some papers into stacks.

"It was a change from the classroom, and that's about the best I can say."

"Dull?"

"Very. Except for lunch. I went off campus to a vegetarian place with Catherine and some others from Conroe, and it was wonderful. They were selling cookbooks, too, and I bought one. We may become vegetarians."

"Fine," Clay said, absently.

"I did make a decision today," Leah said, leaning on his desk. "I decided that I'm suffering from teacher burnout. I've considered it before, but today I was suddenly sure of it."

"You need a rest," said Clay. "I do, too." He stopped and looked up from his papers. "We both have spring vacation next week, Leah. Why couldn't we go on a trip? Let's go to the beach."

"Clay! The nearest beach is six hundred miles away."

"That's all right. We have a week. Why not?"

Leah looked a little bewildered, but she was smiling. "Because, well, for one reason, I'm supposed to work at Maggie's tomorrow."

"Then we'll leave when you get off. We'll go home and pack tonight. We need this, Leah."

"You don't just take off without any planning, without any reservations. Especially on spring break, when all the college students swarm to Florida."

"I'll take care of reservations. I'll get on the phone right now. Somewhere on the coast, there will be a vacancy."

He heard the urgency of his voice, and Leah's wide eyes told him that she heard it, too. She said, "It sounds—well, attractive—but it doesn't make much sense."

"It doesn't have to. I've spent all my life being sensible, but who says everything has to make sense? Right now you and I need a break, and that's a good enough reason for me. What do you say?"

Leah lifted her shoulders and let them fall again, shaking her head, laughing. "Clay, this is so unlike you. I don't know *what* to say."

"You've always liked the beach."

"Yes."

"It'll be nice this time of year. Warm enough, but not hot."

"Yes."

"So, do you want to go? That's all there is to it?"

Leah took a long breath. "Yes," she said, "I want to."

And what do you want, Clay Padgett? I want to love Leah. If I can, that's what I want.

Carmen appeared so suddenly after Leah left that Clay was sure they must have passed each other in the hall.

"Leah dropped by. You just missed her," he said.

"Was that Leah? I could've guessed. She's beautiful. And her timing, I must say, was excellent—or awful, from my point of view." Carmen's tone turned flippant. "Don't worry, though. We met on the steps. She was gone when I got to your door, so she doesn't suspect a thing."

The implication of deceit stabbed at him, and he said, "It's not a small matter, Carmen."

"I'm sorry. Don't scold me."

"I didn't mean to." He rubbed his eyes, gouging the sockets, trying to reach the source of their weariness. "I don't know why you came here just now," he said, "but perhaps it's a good thing."

She held her chin high as she stood in front of his desk. "I came because tonight is opening night, and I couldn't stand the suspense. But I think I wish I hadn't."

Clay looked around on his desk until he found the right envelope, and he tucked the theater pass inside. "I can't," he said, laying it in front of her. "I was a fool to make you think I ever could, or to think so myself. It's pointless to hash it over now, but if I had it to do again and you came to my car with tickets to *Oklahoma!* I'd tell you to run. For both our sakes."

"That's a nice speech, Clay." Carmen's green eyes bore through him. "But you'd like to be talked out of it, wouldn't you?"

"Not this time." He meant it, and his words finally carried the weight of truth, and Carmen, he saw, knew that he meant it.

"You *are* a fool," she said. "You wear your commitments like chains. But I think I said something like that a long time ago, and it didn't do any good."

"If my memory serves me correctly, you said those exact words. And yes, it was a long time ago."

"You're a fool, but I would still change your mind if I could."

"Good-bye, Carmen."

She took the envelope from Clay's desk and slid it into the pocket of her skirt. "If you'll excuse me, I have to pick up an outfit that's being hemmed for tonight. It's Guinevere's costume in the opening scene. White silk."

Clay grinned. Maybe he'd seen her, all along, wearing white silk, long and flowing and queenly. "Bring down the house," he said.

She turned back at the door. "Just tell me. If Leah's timing had been off, if she hadn't shown up here, you would've been there tonight, wouldn't you?"

"No."

Carmen pulled her hair away from her neck and gave it a toss. "How did I know you would say that?"

The water, Leah had already determined, was too cold for swimming, but she was happy enough to lie on the beach. She loved the feel of the sun as her skin soaked it up and baked to a toasty golden brown. Maybe the ultraviolet rays were harmful to skin that tended to burn, but she couldn't believe there was any harm in the dose she was getting. Not when it felt so healthful.

Clay came running out of the waves, shivering. "You had the right idea," he said, grabbing up a towel. "It's a little early for the ocean. But I couldn't see coming all this way and not getting my toes wet."

Leah straightened out his beach towel and held the corners while he sat down. The towels were trying to flap up in the strong breeze off the ocean. Leah felt the fine grit of salt and sand on her fingers, in her hair, even between her teeth. But you didn't worry about that here. At the end of a day in the sun, you showered and scrubbed and came out feeling that you'd lost a whole layer, and it was the cleanest clean there was.

Leah smoothed more oil on her arms. This was their first full day on the beach. If the weather held, she'd go home with a good start on a summer tan, something she hadn't bothered about in years. With a baby you didn't spend much time in the hot sun. With a preschooler you didn't spend much time being still anywhere. She had started teaching T. J. to swim two summers ago and had tanned in the process, but it hadn't seemed important then. Priorities had a way of shifting when you had children. You could build a whole summer around a five-year-old's first uneasy strokes in the water, around his progress from the side of the pool to your fingertips, three feet away. Last summer T. J. would've been swimming. This summer he would've been on his own in the water.

"You ought to try it. It's stimulating. I'll say that."

Leah said, "No thanks. I'll get my toes wet walking along the edge of the water, but I'm not getting wet any higher up than that."

They lay on their towels, both of them slick with oil, and closed their eyes under their sunglasses. With her surroundings blacked out, and against the roar of the waves, Leah found it easy to say what had been on her mind since the teachers' meeting. "I was telling you Friday about being burned out. That's how I've felt this year. Burned out or drained or something. Anyway, it's been a lousy year. I'm ready for a change."

Clay asked, "What do you have left? About eight or nine weeks?"

"I think so. But I'm talking about a real change. I've been toying with the idea of working at Maggie's full time."

Clay was quick to ask, "Was that her suggestion?"

"Not at all," Leah said, maybe with a little too much insistence. "I haven't even talked to her about it, but I know she's looking for an assistant." She'd probably made a mistake in not letting Clay and Maggie get acquainted before now. Somehow he resented Maggie's influence, and Leah was always rushing in to defend her.

Clay was quiet for a moment. Finally he said, "I remember when you applied with the school system and asked for an inner-city school. You're the only teacher I've ever known to make that request."

Leah said, "That was the surest way of getting a job."

"Maybe, but that wasn't why you did it."

"All right. I was younger then, idealistic, naive. Mostly naive. I thought I could change the world."

"You've changed bits and pieces of it, wouldn't you say? Your kids leave you when they're—what? ten? You don't see them when they're twenty-one. But you have to know that some of them, at least, are better off because they spent a year with you."

"I used to believe that. I'd still like to. But the truth is, Conroe Elementary will function just as well without me. Whoever takes my place will do just as well, or better. At this point in my life, I enjoy catering to rich women. So why stay with runny-nosed kids?"

She sat up, and Clay turned on his side and faced her. "Maybe you do need a year off," he said.

"A year, maybe. Or maybe I need a permanent leave." Leah gazed out on the water, not wanting to see disappointment on Clay's face, or perhaps it was not wanting to meet his eyes and face the truth. Not that she was taking an evil path, as opposed to a good one. It was just that her path was leading her farther and farther from Clay's, and they both knew it.

"That's a major decision," he said. "Just be sure that's what you want."

She couldn't say she was sure of anything except that she was burned out. She said, "I'm giving it serious consideration."

"If that's what will make you happy, I hope it works out for you."

Leah couldn't think of any reason why it wouldn't.

Catherine called within the hour of Clay and Leah's arrival home Friday. "I've been trying to reach you all week. Have you been out of town?" she wanted to know. Leah told her about the trip, how they decided at the last minute to go, and tagged it a success. "I think that's marvelous," said Catherine. She sounded bubbly, even for her.

She had called to invite Clay and Leah over to a cookout on Saturday night. Leah, lately, had felt the space between her and Catherine growing colder, and she wondered if the two couples could reclaim any of the easy fun they used to have together. Christmas with the Andersons had been a letdown, even though she'd welcomed the chance to be there instead of her own house. They had all behaved like strangers that evening, but Leah knew that the reason was, in a large part, her. The others were simply waiting to see if she was going to fall apart.

Tomorrow night, she thought, *will be different.* She would tell Catherine what she'd been thinking about resigning; maybe she owed Catherine that much. Whether the four of them kept on seeing each other socially would depend on how this event turned out.

Then she remembered that Maggie was counting on her to work till nine.

"I wish we could, but I have to work." She tried to sound sincere because she was, but she was like the boy who cried wolf. She'd made so many flimsy excuses that now Catherine couldn't believe her when she had a good reason.

"Well, if you're sure you can't make it, we'll do it another time." Of course she didn't believe that. Catherine was just making it easier for her, Leah knew.

But she heard herself say, "How about next Saturday night? Do you have any plans for then?"

"Why, I haven't thought that far ahead, but yes, I'm sure that would be all right." The buoyancy came back into Catherine's voice. "Sure! Next Saturday night will be fine."

"I'll arrange to get off work at five."

"Just come on after that. Ben is taking a group from the church out to Sumner County and they're going to work on building the cabin. But I'm sure he can get back in time to barbecue the steaks."

"Is that the property you and Ben are giving to the church?" Leah remembered vaguely that Clay had mentioned it, but she didn't follow the goings-on at the church very closely these days.

"That's it. We used to think we wanted to live out there someday, but I decided I had enough of the country in North Dakota. The land is beautiful, though. It'll be a nice place for retreats and camp-outs and such."

"And you're building a cabin, too?" Leah wondered at such generosity.

"The church is providing the materials. The guys in the college and career group are doing the work. That's mainly to keep them out of trouble." Her laugh was warm and contagious.

Leah thought of the day that she and Catherine had gone to lunch when they were out of school for snow. She had been cruel to Catherine, without meaning to be, but she had opened a wound, all the same. She wondered, if their roles were reversed, if she could let it pass so easily.

When she began to unpack her suitcase, Leah was caught by the sudden impulse to rearrange all her clothes. Lingerie didn't have to go in the middle drawer, did it? She took all the clothes from the four drawers and threw them on the bed. Piece by piece, she sorted through the pile and filled the drawers again. Then she stood back and looked at her accomplishment. What she had achieved was, in effect, a straighter, neater arrangement of what she'd had before. She had to laugh. Maybe that said something about her. At least she'd be that far ahead if she decided to do spring cleaning this year.

She raised a window and smelled the neighbors' cut grass. Spring, by the calendar, would not arrive until next week, but all the indications were that it was already here. Tree limbs were dotted with tiny green buds. Leah's jonquils and forsythia bushes were eager to bloom; if you looked closely, you could see the yellow sprouts pushing to get out.

For the first time in a year, Leah had the energy and the inclination to ride her bike. In the dark garage, she struggled to wrench the bike from its corner. "I don't blame you," she said out loud to the bike itself. "You haven't been out in so long, you don't know how it feels."

She maneuvered it around the lawn mower, garden tools, and old paint cans, and when she heard the phone, after just getting the bike free, she was tempted not to answer. But she'd never let the phone go unanswered without wondering, for hours, who had called and worrying that it might have been an urgent message.

The caller was Maggie, and Leah was glad to hear her voice. *It must be the weather,* Leah thought. *Everyone sounds a little giddy.*

"This is hardly a conversation to have by phone," Maggie said, "but I was anxious to tell you that I'm finally taking the plunge. You know, that scary plunge into matrimony."

Leah had to let it sink in. "Oh, *that!*" she finally said.

"Aren't you going to wish me well, Leah?"

She stammered. "I'm just so surprised." Surprised was a mild expression. She was jarred.

"I'm a little surprised myself. It just happened. All at once I found myself saying yes."

"I never thought of you as impulsive."

"I didn't mean to imply that I'd never given marriage any thought. You know I have." She began to sound more like Maggie. "I didn't deny loving Alan, but I couldn't let go of my hard-boiled independence. Now that's not how I think of it at all. Independence isn't far down the road from loneliness." She laughed. "Just listen to this. In one short week, I've become a babbling romantic. I'm even going to be a June bride."

Leah couldn't keep from catching a germ of Maggie's cheerfulness. "Tell me. Did this romantic engagement come about by phone?"

"Oh, no. Alan's been here. He came unexpectedly and made a wonderful speech that fell just short of being an ultimatum. Ordinarily, if I'm given an either-or, I'll take the *or*, just for spite. But in this case, it would've meant not seeing Alan again, and suddenly that made an impact. You know the old saying about not seeing the forest for the trees. I can tell you, Leah, some of us who pride ourselves on our vision tend to be remarkably blind."

It occurred to Leah, the moment she hung up, that she had forgotten to ask a basic question. When she arrived at work the next morning, she asked.

"The shop? Yes, I meant to tell you," said Maggie. "My father is sure he can find a buyer, soon after the wedding, if not before. Alan and I have talked it over. I'd like to try my luck with the same kind of boutique in New York, and with Alan's connections, it just might work. I'll miss you, Leah. Are you sure you don't want to move to New York?"

15

The children came back from spring vacation clamoring about the end of school as if they had already signed off for the year, and the remaining days were no more than a postscript. Some were already making calendars so they could mark off each day. Danny was one whose enthusiasm dwindled when he realized how many squares were involved in his calendar. "*How* many days?" he cried out when Emily informed him that eight weeks did indeed equal forty school days. Danny wadded up his paper and stuck his ruler back in his desk, mumbling that marking off days wouldn't make them go any faster, anyway.

Leah took a firm stand early in the day when Corey put on his baseball glove during math class. She announced that school would be in session for eight more weeks, which translated into forty school days, and that there was plenty of work to be done. She was not at all sure that she had prepared her motley crew for the fifth grade. If eight weeks seemed interminable to the children, it seemed far too short a time for Leah to accomplish what she had failed to do throughout the year.

Her speech served to get the whole group on task for that moment, but Leah could sense that the majority only feigned interest in dividing fractions. Only a few had their hearts in it, a few girls like Emily and Lisa.

Edward continued to amaze Leah. Throughout the morning, he worked as diligently as most of the other students, which wasn't saying much for the others but was saying a lot for Edward. It was obvious that behind the scowl had been a quick mind, all along. The glazed stare had been deceptive. Although Edward rarely appeared to be paying attention, he had somehow absorbed a lot of what had been taught during the year. For the past few weeks, he had been turning in his assignments and making average grades. His work indicated a large dose of ability, if not much effort. On tests, he correctly answered questions that depended on using common sense or listening in class. If studying beforehand was required to answer a question, Edward was out of luck. He also missed quite a bit by being absent, although his attendance had improved somewhat since cold weather. He was doing well enough to get by, but still, could he handle fifth grade? Only eight weeks to work on his skills. Leah had her work cut out.

Lunch break released the dynamo that the children had sat on all morning. They chattered in falsetto, picked and poked at each other with hands that seemed to have no connection to their brains, and squirmed so that the line going and coming from the cafeteria looked like one large wiggly worm.

After lunch, the children had trouble settling in their seats, and when they did, a restless current continued to stir in the room. Spring fever, Leah guessed, and she could hardly blame the students when her own eyes were drawn, just as theirs were, to the sunshine playing on the tender new leaves that brushed against the window.

"Let's rest a few minutes before we get into our science lesson," said Leah, settling behind her desk. She opened the big file drawer at her right and reached for the folder labeled "Poems to Read Aloud." The limp folder was a little ragged around the edges, but it had served her well through the years. She spread out the contents on her desk and thumbed through the pages for poems that had been favorites of previous classes.

"Just put your head on your desk, or sit quietly, and let me share some poems with you," said Leah. Then she began to read:

I'll tell you how the sun rose,—
A ribbon at a time.
The steeples swam in amethyst,
The news like squirrels ran.

The hills untied their bonnets,
The bobolinks begun.
Then I said softly to myself,
"That must have been the sun!"

From the first, the soft, rhythmic patterns brought a hush to the room, and the fidgeting bodies became still. Leah went on:

Whisky, frisky
Hippity hop,
Up he goes
To the tree top!

Shirly, twirly,
Round and round,
Down he scampers
To the ground.

Furly, curly
What a tail!
Tall as a feather
Broad as a sail!

Then she chose a poem for pure humor:

Multiplication is vexation,
Division is as bad;
The Rule of Three doth puzzle me,
And Practice drives me mad.

The children did not take their eyes off Leah, and they seemed to breathe only between poems. Leah kept mostly to the poems written in a lighter vein, and poems with a heavy beat, but she could not resist one of her own favorites:

I must go down to the seas again, to the lonely sea and the sky,
And all I ask is a tall ship and a star to steer her by.
And the wheel's kick and the wind's song and the white
    sail's shaking,
And a gray mist on the sea's face, and a gray dawn
    breaking.

She was sure that at least one student would appreciate the lovely imagery, and the enchantment written on Emily's face proved her right.

After twenty-five minutes, Leah said, "This poem is the last one for today," and a chorus of groans went up in the room. Leah read:

Brown and furry
Caterpillar, in a hurry
Take your walk
To the shady leaf or stalk

. . . .

May no toad spy you,
May the little birds pass by you;
Spin and die,
To live again a butterfly.

"Now," she said, "does anyone know why I ended with that one?"

A few hands went up. Leah nodded to Lisa, who said, timidly, "Probably because we're going to have science now."

"And we're studying metamorphis!" Danny added.

"Meta-mor-pho-sis," Leah said. "Right."

"Please, can we have poems again tomorrow?" asked Emily.

"Yes, in fact," Leah thought for a moment and said, "I was planning to start a poetry unit next week in language arts. I don't see any reason why we can't start it tomorrow."

"What will we have to do?" asked Corey.

Leah explained that they would study different kinds of poems, different subjects, rhythms, and poets. The students would write poetry, too. Then each one would make a booklet of favorite poems and poems of their own.

Lisa raised her hand and frowned. "We've had to write poems before. I can't make good rhymes."

"The lines don't have to rhyme," Leah explained. "We're going to read a lot of poetry that doesn't rhyme. We'll read poems on all kinds of subjects. Anything that's on your mind can become a poem." She added, "And everyone has a poem in him."

"Can't we start today?" asked Teresa.

"I have to pay a visit to the library first," said Leah, "to check out all the resource materials that we'll need."

"In a way, we've already started," said Emily. For her, it was true. She had already started scribbling the beginning of a poem.

The pattern was the same each day. The students grew increasingly restless as the morning went by, and their excitement peaked at lunchtime. After lunch, when Leah managed to get them settled enough to start class, they worked on the poetry unit. The poetry affected them like a tranquilizer, and they were usually quiet and receptive when science class followed.

On Friday, the level of noise throughout the whole school rose a couple of decibels. As Leah led her wiggly line back from lunch, she was already wondering if poetry could possibly have a calming effect today. Suddenly, just outside the room, the line disintegrated and the whispers became shouts.

"Mrs. Padgett! Quick! A fight!"

Edward and a boy named Terrence Rucker were scrambling on the floor. Leah managed to get them apart, only because Terrence pulled back when she said, "Stop! Stop it right now!" Edward showed no intention of stopping, and Leah had to hold his arms. "Come on, Edward, calm down," she said. His arms were still tense, and she had the feeling that if she turned loose, he would dive into Terrence again.

Terrence, who had been eager to get out of the fight, now said bravely, "You better keep away from me or I'll tear you apart!"

Corey came to Terrence's side. "Edward hit him for nothin', Mrs. Padgett! Terrence just told him he saw his mama in the shopping center, that's all."

"You didn't see her!" Edward spat at Terrence.

"I did, *too!*"

"All right, all right, we'll get to the bottom of this later. Children, get inside the room, please."

The students meandered toward the door. Several came up to volunteer information before they went inside. "Corey's right. Edward jumped on Terrence." "It was all Edward's fault." "Edward pounced on Terrence for nothin'!"

In the middle of the confusion, Mr. Carlton happened by. "What's going on?" he asked, but his piercing eyes settled on Terrence and Edward, and it was obvious that he had sized up the situation.

"I think everything's under control," said Leah.

"Do these young men need to go to my office?" Mr. Carlton continued to eye the offenders with disapproval.

"I believe Terrence can go on in the room," said Leah. "I need to talk with Edward. He can wait in your office until I get my class working."

With a knowing look, Mr. Carlton said, "I'll stay with your class while you take care of this."

"Do you mind?"

"Go ahead." He managed a half-smile. "It hasn't been so long that I don't know what to do in a classroom."

Leah tried to plan, on the way to the office, what approach she would take with Edward. She glanced down at the angry child beside her, knowing that the progress they had made in the past weeks was in jeopardy.

Strategy proved to be useless. The moment the door was closed behind them in Mr. Carlton's office, Edward cried out, "He's a liar! He didn't see my mama at no shopping center!"

Leah knelt beside him. "I want to help, Edward, but I don't understand."

His nostrils twitched, and his breathing quickened.

"Please, tell me—what is all of this about your mother?"

The words burst out of him. "She's gone! She's *been* gone!"

There was a moment when the sound seemed to echo off the walls, and Edward looked as shocked by his words as Leah was. Then he let his chin fall to his chest, and his whole body slumped. Leah could almost see the anger drain out of him.

"I'm sorry, Edward. I didn't know."

He said in a small, thin voice, "She left us last summer. I don't know why."

Leah reached for his sagging shoulders. *My baby is gone, and I hurt, too, and I wonder if it will ever stop. I know, Edward. I know.*

She hugged him, and he didn't resist.

Mr. Carlton didn't speak to Leah about the incident when she returned to the room. All he said to her was, "These children are writing some wonderful poetry." He handed Danny's paper back to him and said, "Good job, Son." Then he left.

Danny held the paper up to Leah. "Read it, Mrs. Padgett. I wrote it all by myself."

She scanned the poem:

> Baseball games are lots of fun,
> The coach is a good friend,
> He tells us to enjoy the game,
> Whether we lose or win.

Catching fly balls and grounders
Is really a lot of fun,
But the best part is batting,
And making a winning run.

"Very nice, Danny," said Leah, and when she looked up, a half dozen other students were crowding around, wanting her to read their poems. "All right," she said, moving to her desk, "one at a time." The group followed her, encircling her desk, leaning on their elbows.

"All I want to know," said Emily, "is can you think of a two-syllable word that means 'win'?"

"Win? Two syllables? Hm-m-m. How about 'succeed'?"

Emily thought about it and said, "That won't exactly work."

"Have you tried the dictionary?"

She looked a little sheepish. "I was just going to."

Leah skimmed through two poems about dogs and had just finished the second about spring when Edward came into the room. He had asked permission to go by the rest room, and Leah had considered saying something to the class while he was out, but the opportunity hadn't come.

The students watched him come in, and then they went on about their business. Edward had been in trouble many times, and it wasn't unusual to see him slip in from the office. He went straight to his seat. For a few moments, he looked out the window. Then he opened his notebook and began to write.

Since the students were busy with their original poems, Leah let them work through science class. Lisa brought up her poem and smiled as she said, "It doesn't rhyme, but I like it."

Most of the students finished writing their poems and started putting their booklets together, decorating the construction paper covers with crayons. Leah announced that she would take up the complete booklets on Monday, and Emily's face showed relief. She was poring over the dictionary. "I want my poem to have pretty words," she whispered, as Leah passed her desk.

Time came for PE. While the students buzzed around the room, putting away their supplies, Leah noticed that Terrence and Edward were eyeing each other. As they came to the front to line up, Terrence said suddenly, "He'd better leave me alone, Mrs. Padgett."

"Please don't start again, Terrence," said Leah.

"*I'm* not startin' anything."

Edward laid a sheet of paper on Leah's desk without saying a word.

"Edward was wrong to fight," said Leah, "and we aren't going to have any more fighting because it doesn't solve anything. At the same time, you shouldn't say things to people that might hurt them or make them angry."

"I thought he'd like to know his mama was still in town," said Terrence. "I didn't mean nothin'." He shifted his eyes from Leah to Edward, who returned a cold glare.

Danny snickered, "Terrence is scared."

The whole class seemed to be listening now. Leah felt a dull ache at her temples. Why couldn't they just leave the matter alone? Edward would be all right if they just wouldn't talk about it.

Emily, who had been making the final copy of her poem, now placed her paper with Edward's, on Leah's desk. Then she walked up to Edward and said, "Everybody knows things about their family that they aren't proud of. If you weren't so silly about it, nobody would think much about your mama."

And to Terrence she made a face of disgust. "You're sillier than *he* is, Terrence Rucker. His family is none of your business."

Edward and Terrence, both having been told off by a girl, made half-hearted grins at each other. Emily joined the end of the line and said, as she passed Leah, "I finished my poem. I hope you think it's pretty."

When the students were finally gone, Leah picked up the two papers on her desk. On the first one, uneasy fingers had rolled the corners and pressed them out, again and again, and the writing was a mixture of cursive and manuscript. Leah read the small, crowded words:

> I like my little brother,
> He thinks I'm real big,
> When he gets skinned,
> I wash the dirt off,
> I wake him up when he has dreams
> That make him scream,
> I have to be big for him,
> I wish I had a big brother, too.

The other page was crisp. The poem was centered, and the handwriting was right out of the cursive manual. The words jumped off the page at Leah:

> Nature's promise makes it so,
> Fields of green come after snow,
> On the coldest winter day,
> Spring is never far away.
> Rain clouds move aside for sun,
> Morning comes when night is done,
> Right will triumph over wrong,
> Silent earth gives forth a song.

Leah was glad that Edward and Emily were not leaning on her desk, waiting for her to respond. She would praise them appropriately when they returned, but at that moment, she couldn't have spoken a word.

16

The alarm clock was on Ben's side of the bed, but it was Catherine who woke him. "You didn't hear the alarm? It's 6:30." Her voice sounded muddy, coming to him through his sleepy fog.

"Just five more minutes." He rolled over.

"You'll never get to the church by 7:30."

It registered now that this was the Saturday he'd committed to working on the cabin in Sumner County. Fifteen kids, maybe as many as twenty, would be at the church in an hour, counting on him. He sat up and swung his legs off onto the floor. "I'm tired just thinking about it."

"Thinking about what?"

"All the sawing and hammering and carrying lumber. I'll let the guys do all the work."

"I'll bet."

Catherine made a bigger breakfast than he wanted or had time for, but he always managed to clean his plate. He'd picked up that habit in the Marines, when you ate every bite you could get because you didn't know when the next meal would happen or what the circumstances would be.

"You're right on schedule," Catherine said. "You're not going to be late." So Ben slowed down on his last bites. Catherine was always fussing at him about eating too fast.

"You're not eating anything," he said, indicating the scrambled eggs on her plate.

She made a face. "Toast is about all I can get down this morning."

"You've got to keep up your strength," he told her in a serious, fatherly voice that made her laugh.

"Yes, Dr. Anderson."

Ben was doing fine timewise until George Kirby called.

"I just wanted to let you know that I'm not going," George said, "so don't wait for me."

"What is it, George?" Ben asked. "Is something wrong?"

"I feel lousy. I don't think anyone would want me around today."

Ben made an effort to keep his voice even. "Are you sick?" George always made you work to get any answers from him, and it was like pulling teeth. But if you didn't go through the process, you ran the risk of making George think you didn't care, and right now what George needed most was to know that he was important to someone.

"I'm not sick, just sick of the whole mess. School and everything."

"What hapened?"

He finally got around to explaining that he'd met with a counselor in financial aids yesterday and talked about his chances for a scholarship next year. His last quarter's grades had fallen. Right at exam time, he'd blown everything, he said. Well, he hadn't flunked out, but he'd dropped below the 3.0 average that a scholarship student was supposed to maintain.

"Can't you work on bringing up your average this quarter?" Ben asked. "You have a class under Clay Padgett, don't you? He says you're one of his best students."

"I'll make a good grade in Dr. Padgett's class, and I'm counting on a good quarter all around. The trouble is, they're already deciding who's going to get the scholarships for next year. The guy in financial aids just as much as told me I was out. Even if I make a 4.0 this time, they'll probably already have their money given out."

"Did the counselor say that?"

"Not exactly. He gave me the standard line: Fill out the forms, and the committee will review my situation."

Ben saw Catherine pointing toward her watch.

"Look, George," he said, "let's talk about this again sometime today. I hate to see you not come along with us just because you're kind of down. It'll do you good to get out there with the other guys. What do you say?"

"I don't think I'd be very good company."

"Sure you will. Come on. We need you."

George seemed to be thinking about it. "I might," he said, "but don't wait for me."

Ben had a feeling George would show up, and he did, just in time. But he hadn't exaggerated the mood he was in. He was down, lower than Ben had ever seen him, and Ben wondered as the day went on if it hadn't been a mistake to insist that George come along.

He did the work, although perhaps not his share, but there was a sullenness in his face, the scowl of someone with a migraine. He didn't have much to say, even to Bruce, who had become a good friend. A couple of times Ben heard him snap "I'm busy!" when someone wanted him for something, and then he noticed that the other guys just left him alone.

The work went fast. Ben and Catherine had started building the cabin some years ago when they thought it would be nice to have a place to get away to for a weekend or a week in the summer. The trouble was, they hardly ever had a free weekend. If they weren't busy at the church, there was yard work or some other pressing project around the house, or some function in Nashville that they wanted to attend. When it came to vacation-time, they liked to get farther away than forty-five miles. So they never got the cabin built. They had both decided that the land wasn't going to be used unless they gave it to the church.

Today the guys were framing. Although they called it a cabin, the building was actually going to be more like a small, crude house. One of the guys, named Kenny, had done a lot of work with his dad, who was a house builder, so he was a real help. Every time Ben stood back and looked at their accomplishment, he nodded appreciatively. The place was beginning to have some form, and in a way it was like his own dream taking shape.

Toward the end of the day, Ben missed George and asked where he was. No one seemed to know or care. Ben figured he'd just taken a break, but after a half hour, he still hadn't come back. "Are you sure you didn't see him go off?" Ben asked Bruce.

Bruce hadn't seen him leave, but when he got to thinking, he remembered the last time he'd seen him. "We were talking about Darryl changing schools. He's been accepted at Vanderbilt. Somebody said, 'It'll be a lot more expensive,' and Darryl said, 'They'll probably give me a full scholarship.' He was just kidding. We all laughed, but I remember looking at George, wondering if he was laughing, because he's always worrying about losing his scholarship, and he gave me a dirty look. He got up from that corner where he was hammering and went over to get some more nails. I *thought* he was getting more nails, but now I can't say for sure. I never actually saw him after that. Maybe he did go outside."

Kenny said, "I can't imagine even George being so touchy," but Ben could. He looked at the dwindling pile of materials and told the guys that they could start winding up. He checked his watch. He needed to get on back and take a hot shower before time to start barbecuing. He figured they were all ready to call it a day.

He shouted George's name, and some of the others called for him, too, but there was no answer. "I'll try up at the waterfall," Ben said, finally. That was the only clear path around. All the rest was wooded, with a lot of underbrush and snakes, too, this time of year, although George wouldn't consider that if he'd had the urge to go stomping out there. To be as intelligent as George was, sometimes he showed very little sense.

"Do you want me to go?" asked Bruce.

"No, I'd better." Ben regretted that he hadn't had a chance to talk with George during the day, but there never had been an opportunity. Maybe that was one thing that was bothering George. Maybe he was feeling neglected. And maybe Ben could smooth over his ruffled feathers. If he didn't grab him and shake him till he rattled first.

"We'll have everything ready to go when you get back," said Kenny.

"Thanks." Ben's eyes made a sweep of the path that led straight up the hill, and then he shook his head and grinned. He guessed he was getting old. The hill looked like a mountain.

George knew he shouldn't have left the group. He had known it almost before he'd set foot on the path, but once he had made a fool of himself by running off, he couldn't make himself go back.

He sat on a big flat rock and let his feet dangle out over the drop-off. The waterfall itself was a smooth cascade no more than four feet wide, not a breathtaking plunge of turbulent white water. But the drop-off was steep. *A good place for a suicide,* George thought, *if one were so inclined.* He had never been inclined, himself. In spite of his frequent bouts with despair, he never kidded himself about the attractiveness of ending it all. He guessed wanting to live was a sign that there was hope for him. Maybe.

But sometimes he did wish that it were possible to drop out of life for a little while, take a rest from living, just a temporary one, when it all got to weighing down on him, like today. He wished he hadn't let Ben talk him into coming with them. He'd wanted to please Ben, but when he got moody, the way he was now, he did stupid things, like running off when the guys got to talking about scholarships. He couldn't even remember exactly what they'd said—oh, yeah, Darryl had said he could get a scholarship any time he wanted it, or something like that. That didn't have anything to do with *him*. He knew that. But it made him boil, all at once. It was that same kind of blind anger that hits you when a guy cuts in front of you in traffic.

He drew up his knee and tied his tennis shoe. The falls, small as it was, made a gentle roar that drowned out the crackle of footsteps on twigs, but when George changed positions, he caught a glimpse of someone approaching. He heard, "So here's where you are," just as he turned to see Ben.

George couldn't look him in the eye, but he said, "I knew I should be getting back. I guess everybody's ready to leave."

Ben was breathing hard. "Next time you decide to leave without letting us know, pick a level place to go."

George wasn't sure how to take that until he looked up and saw the sideways grin that made Ben such an easy person to like. George wished sometimes that Ben *weren't* so likable. He didn't deserve for anybody like Ben to take an interest in him.

"Yeah, I shouldn't have left," he said. "I got up tight about something or other that wasn't even important. Then I figured the guys were down there laughing at me."

"Those guys are your friends, George, just like me. You've got to trust *people*, George. Most of them aren't half bad if you'll give them a chance."

Ben was really short of breath now, and George felt a creeping fear that something was wrong, something bad. "Maybe you should sit down, Ben," he said.

"Good idea," and Ben immediately leaned against the nearest tree and sort of slid down its trunk, holding across his middle with his other hand.

"I'll get some water for you to splash on your face." George was beginning to feel panicky, weak in the pit of his stomach. He never had been good in a crisis. But he knelt down by the falls and cupped his hands, getting as much water as he could hold, as quickly as he could. When he turned around, full-blown panic held him still. The water trickled between his fingers as he cried, "Please, God, no!"

Catherine kept checking her watch. "I can't imagine what's keeping Ben," she said.

"You know how it is with a group of guys," said Leah. "You can't get everybody ready to leave at the same time, or you get ten miles down the road, and one remembers that he left his wallet, and you have to go back."

"Or," said Clay, "they may have just kept working, trying to get to a stopping place, until it was later than they realized."

"Probably so," said Catherine, absently. "Let's go on and start the steaks. Surely Ben will be here by the time they're done. Clay, how about doing the honors?"

"Sure." He slipped on Ben's apron and chef's hat. Ben always made a big production out of barbecuing, so Clay tried to put on a good act. He balanced the platter of red T-bones high overhead and affected a thick accent. "Ladies, the master chef will now prepare a culinary wonder, steak a la Padgett." He swooped over to the counter and gathered the utensils for barbecuing, cradling the bowl of barbecue sauce next to him in the bend of his arm, and did a little dance to the outside. It wasn't his style, really, but he was glad to see the women smile. So far, the evening was a little tense.

The heat radiated from the grill, and each steak hit the rack with a sizzle. Clay heard a car in the driveway. He closed the top of the grill and went around the corner of the house to greet Ben. But he saw Reverend Kent instead.

"Clay," said Reverend Kent, "I didn't know you were here, but I'm certainly glad you are."

Clay felt the weight of his voice. "Is something wrong?" he asked.

"I just had some bad news, Clay. I got a call from the boys who were with Ben, out in the country. It seems that Ben has had a heart attack. At least that's what they thought. The boys who gave me the information were pretty shaken, and they had just called the ambulance."

"How bad is it?"

"Bad, I think."

They went inside, where Leah was tossing a salad and

Catherine was buttering a loaf of homemade bread. Clay let Reverend Kent do the talking. Bad news, heart attack, ambulance, hospital—Clay felt each word slap him in the face. He watched Catherine and Leah inhale the news, thinking maybe they would need some sort of support, but the only reaction he saw was one moment of alarm in Leah's eyes, and from Catherine, a breathless flurry of activity. "Let's get to the hospital," she said, turning off the oven. "Just let me get my purse. Leah, yours is on that chair. Clay, you'd better put out the fire," and when he hesitated, because the words didn't sink in, she added, "on the grill, on the *grill*."

They left the house in less than five minutes. Clay and Leah took their car. Catherine rode with Reverend Kent. "Lucky we're following," said Clay, as they pulled out of the subdivision. "I didn't even think to ask which hospital."

Leah didn't say anything.

"I'm afraid we're in for something very serious," he said. "Are you going to be all right?"

She spoke for the first time since she'd heard about Ben. "I feel like I'm reliving a nightmare," she said.

17

The emergency room was quiet when they entered, hushed, almost. *As quiet as death*, Leah thought. The odor of antiseptic was so sharp that she could taste it. She swallowed and felt queasy. Clay had been right. This was something serious. She could feel it.

At first, the room looked empty, but a man in hospital greens appeared behind the glass at the nurse's station, and as they started in his direction, someone called Reverend Kent's name.

"Kenny and Bruce," the pastor said, guiding Catherine toward them. "What's the situation?" he asked.

Leah remembered Kenny, and he was the one who answered. "We don't know. We haven't heard anything since we came, but it's only been a few minutes. We were right behind the ambulance, but you almost beat us here."

"Maybe we can find out something from them," said Clay, indicating the nurses' station. Now there were two other nurses in sight, talking to each other, smiling. Didn't they know what was going on? Leah wondered. Or were they so calloused from working in life-death situations that they didn't bother to notice anymore?

There was a row of seats, alternating blue and beige, and Reverend Kent insisted that Catherine and Leah sit down. The boys came over to Catherine, and Bruce sat beside her, while Kenny squatted in front of her, as they tried to explain what had happened.

Ben had gone up the hill to find George Kirby. A few minutes later George had come running back to the group, saying that Ben must've had a heart attack. A couple of guys drove to the nearest telephone to call an ambulance and Reverend Kent, while the rest went up the mountain. They didn't dare move Ben until the paramedics came.

"But he was breathing?" Catherine asked in a shaky voice.

"Yes, and he tried to talk," Kenny said, "but we kept telling him not to, and the paramedics said the same thing when they got there."

"It seemed to take forever," Bruce said, frowning, shaking his head. His voice had a dreamy air to it, as if he were trying to remember something from long ago. "If we could've just got him here faster, he would've had a better chance."

Reverend Kent was quick to say, "As far as I can see, every move you made was right."

"But it took so long." Bruce couldn't seem to get the idea out of his system. "We shouldn't have let him go after George in the first place. If George hadn't run off. . . . "

Reverend Kent stepped in again. "Try not to worry about all that. It's behind you now."

Clay came back from talking with one of the nurses, but she hadn't been able to tell him any more than they knew. For a few minutes they all sat on the hard, colored seats, saying little except in the way of small talk, and that was mostly between Reverend Kent and the boys. Where was the van? The guys took it on back to the church. How much work did they get done on the cabin? They used up most of the materials.

"Do you think it's going to be much longer?" Bruce asked, finally.

"There's no way of telling," said Reverend Kent.

"Should we stay?"

"I don't think that's necessary."

Leah saw relief in both boys' faces.

"If you think we should, . . . " Kenny let his voice trail off.

"I'll let you know what we find out. Go ahead."

They had barely disappeared when a new face appeared in the glass enclosure. Leah nudged Clay and said, "A doctor." Something about the exchange between the man and the nurses told her that he was not only a doctor, but Ben's doctor. Then all of the group behind the glass looked out at the group in the chairs, and Leah's blood ran cold.

Catherine and Reverend Kent had noticed him, too, and they started to stand as the doctor came their way, but he held up his hand in a quieting motion and said softly, "Please, keep your seats. You're the Anderson family?"

"I'm Mrs. Anderson," said Catherine, in a voice that sounded too reasonable, Leah thought, for the occasion.

Reverend Kent got up, gesturing for the doctor to sit beside Catherine, and he did. He was a young man, perhaps younger than any of them, but his strong, weathered face had encountered enough suffering to give him authenticity. Leah could see it. He had been through this before. He was a person you could trust. For an instant she told herself, *Everything will be all right.*

"I'm sorry, Mrs. Anderson," he said. "We did everything we could, but we couldn't save his life."

It was Leah who wailed, "No, no, *no*," spilling her purse out on the floor, sending coins rolling to the other side of the room.

He was a patient doctor, more than most, Leah thought. He had performed his grim assignment. Now he could get by with excusing himself, but he didn't. He waited out the blow with Catherine, just sitting in silence, until she was able to ask, "Was it a heart attack?"

"Yes, a massive coronary," he said. "We never had a chance with him. But it may be some comfort to know that he went peacefully, without a struggle. I've seen a lot of deaths, Mrs. Anderson, and it doesn't always happen that way."

"You were with him at the very last?" Catherine asked.

"Yes, I was."

"Did he say anything?"

The doctor considered for a minute. "Yes, when I first got to him, he was saying something about flying."

"Thank you," said Catherine, and she smiled.

There were matters that had to be taken care of, calls to make, forms to sign. While they waited, a screaming ambulance brought in two victims of a car accident. A child came out with her arm in a cast. The doctor who, earlier, had watched Ben die, now winked and waved at the little girl as she left with her mother.

"We can take Catherine home," said Clay.

"I'll be glad to go with you, Catherine, if you need me." Reverend Kent took the seat beside her again. "You can stay the night at our house if it would be easier for you."

"She can stay with us," Leah said. Her voice sounded raspy and unfamiliar, even to herself.

"Thanks, but I want to go home. I'll be all right," said Catherine. She looked down at her hands, pressing at her knuckles. "I don't understand how it happened. I thought he was in good health. He was a young man, well, too young to die."

Reverend Kent was supposed to be the man with the answers, Leah thought, and she waited to hear how he might console Catherine, how he might interpret why Ben had to die. But he shook his head. Leah watched the skin knot up between his eyebrows, and she thought that, all at once, he looked old and very tired. She kept waiting. Surely he kept a pat answer on hand for a moment like this. Surely his ministry required that he rehearse a line or two for such occasions.

As if he'd read Leah's thoughts, he said, "I'm a little like the doctor, Catherine. I've been in this spot a lot of times. It never gets any easier, but this has to be the hardest." He took out a handkerchief and wiped the corners of his eyes. "Ben was a good friend. I loved him."

Then he stood up and cleared his throat. "Catherine, promise me you'll let me know if I can help in any way."

"I will. I'll talk to you tomorrow about the funeral."

He turned to Leah. "You can be a lot of help to her," he said.

"I'll try."

Reverend Kent exchanged a few words with Clay, and then he left. He was a tall, commanding figure of authority. He was probably wise, too. But he didn't have any answers about death. He hadn't even made a stab at answering *why*, and that surprised Leah. She'd somehow expected him to explain it away in lofty theological language. Was that why she'd brushed him off all these months when he'd wanted to talk with her? Maybe it was. Maybe she'd been afraid he would tell her T. J. was better off in heaven, or that T. J. had to die to satisfy some mysterious will of God. Worst of all, what if Reverend Kent had told her that the Maker of the Universe had more important considerations than the life of one six-year-old boy? If he'd made her believe that, she would've had to sacrifice everything she'd ever believed about the God who knows when a sparrow falls. Maybe that had been behind it all, the fear that she *would* understand why God had taken her child, and understanding, she could never love him.

At Catherine's house, the wilted salad still sat on the kitchen counter, along with the loaf of bread—half of it sliced—and a stick of butter, melted out of shape.

"I'll see what I left outside," said Clay. "I did put the steaks in the refrigerator, but nothing else."

Catherine looked at the food on the counter. "We left in a hurry. I wonder if I can save any of this stuff." She picked up a soft, drooping leaf of lettuce and plopped it into her mouth, making a face. "If I hadn't already doused it with oil and vinegar, it might be worth keeping."

"Let me make some coffee," said Leah. That sounded like a useful contribution. She'd felt, otherwise, useless. Clay seemed to know what ought to be done, and even Catherine had a better sense of it than she did. "Yes, I can make coffee." She opened what she thought was the coffee canister, but it held sugar instead.

"There's a jar of the decaffeinated kind in that cabinet," said Catherine, pointing. "Let's just heat some water for that." She filled the teapot with water herself.

Clay brought a full tray from outside, and Catherine put away the barbecue sauce and clean utensils. Then they all sat at the kitchen table, and Leah noticed that the three of them wrapped their hands around their coffee mugs in the same way. Maybe it was just the need they all had to hold on to something right now, and the cups were warm and steamy. Catherine was already talking about the funeral, making plans. Leah wondered how she could concentrate on those details, so soon after the shock of Ben's death. *You don't have to think about it now,* Leah wanted to say, but she couldn't seem to say anything.

"Do you need to let some family members know about this?" Clay asked. A good question. Leah was glad he could take charge. She guessed he'd made all the arrangements for T. J.'s funeral by himself. She couldn't remember.

"Ben does have a sister in San Diego." Catherine looked at her watch. "She's a nurse, and she's worked the three to eleven shift for years. Unless this just happens to be her night off, I won't get her until eleven-thirty, San Diego time."

"Any other family?"

"That's about it."

"How about the people at the flying service? Could I call them for you tomorrow?"

"Tomorrow? What day is this, Saturday? Well, yes, I guess you could do that. There's someone out there every day. I'll give you a name." She found a memo pad and wrote a name and number with the bold, neat penmanship of a fourth-grade teacher. "Today's Saturday, and if I go to the funeral home in the morning, I can arrange to have the funeral Monday. Don't you think so? Back in Coreen, people talked about the dead 'laying a corpse.' My uncle lay a corpse for three days, which was supposed to be a proper waiting period before the funeral, I guess. I remember because Aunt Harriet was like a walking corpse herself by the time she'd mourned with everyone in Coreen for three days. I don't think I could stand that." Taking a breath, she said, "I know I'm rambling."

"Do you need us to take you to the funeral home in the morning?" Clay asked.

"No, thanks. I can handle it."

"You're sure you don't need someone to stay with you tonight?"

"I'm sure. I appreciate what you've done, but there's no reason for you to stay any longer."

"We haven't done anything," Leah said, at last, as they moved toward the kitchen door. "I wish . . . I don't know. I just feel helpless."

"So do I," said Catherine.

What she did wish was that her mind would start clicking for her again, and then, maybe, she *could* do something. Reverend Kent had told Leah that she could help Catherine, and that ought to be true. But what did she have to offer her? What, for that matter, did Catherine *need*? The strong ones, like Catherine and Clay, didn't really need anything from the weaklings like her.

No, she told herself, *I shouldn't think that way*. It was wrong to resent what was good in Clay and Catherine, but where did they get such powerful doses of endurance, anyway? She brushed her teeth, brushed her hair, threw her dirty clothes in the hamper, flipped off the bathroom light. She was going through motions, but none of it seemed real. She had the strange feeling that she was moving through a fog, like the fog that had wrapped itself around her when T. J. died. It had been a year, almost exactly a year. Did Clay realize that? Did anyone else remember? The paramedics who rushed T. J. to the hospital and saw him pronounced dead upon arrival? Did they ever think of him now? The neighbors who gathered in the street? The children in T. J.'s class? Jeremy Dylan, who found the red jacket in the ditch?

Leah moved into the dark bedroom, dark, but for the pale light of a silver quarter moon—an apple slice, T. J. used to call it. The fog, or the darkness—or her own sorrow, perhaps—hung so thick that Leah held her hands out in front of her to cut her way through. For a moment, she thought she might smother, but she wouldn't take the chance of waking Clay by turning on a light. She could make out his shape in the bed. He was lying on his stomach, his hands clasped above his head, his chin in the pillow. That was a favorite position. He would get a good night's rest. She envied him for it. No, she hated him for it.

Leah felt the jacket before she saw it. It was a crinkled ball, crammed in the corner of the drawer since the last time, but the jacket took shape on her knees, and she ironed it smooth with her hand. If T. J. was no longer alive in anyone else's memory, he had to be in hers.

"Leah."

Clay's voice was not unkind, not accusing, and there was no question implied as to what she was doing, kneeling there at the open drawer. The word—her name—came across as a simple acknowledgment: *I'm here.* But the voice, floating on the darkness, was unexpected, and Leah jerked, like a child caught marking on the walls. She held the jacket against her, looking toward the shadow, which was Clay, moving out of bed. "I don't care if you see. I don't care," she said, but with the words rose a sob in her throat. Then something rushed from her, a wild force like a tiger unleashed. She clasped her arms around herself, trying to hold herself *in.* Was this the breakdown that everyone had waited for? It must be. Her mind and body split into two separate entities, and all the restraints that her mind had willed counted for nothing now, as her body took its own course, heaving in great convulsions, making cries like a wounded animal. Maybe she *was* wounded. In the dark she couldn't see, but was it blood gushing? Was it life, pouring from her? No, it couldn't be. It was just the breakdown everyone had expected, only breakdown wasn't the right word. You didn't fall apart; you turned yourself inside out.

"Leah." He said it again, maybe over and over, or perhaps the word echoed. She couldn't tell, but her name kept vibrating in her ears. Then she felt Clay's arms, pulling her to him, felt him whisper into her hair: "You never cried one tear, the whole time." And at last she understood what was happening to her. Maybe it wasn't so bizarre after all, because Clay kept saying, "It's all right, it's all right," as he held her, rocking her back and forth until they were both wet and salty.

Where did all the tears come from anyway? She couldn't stop. Great waves passed through her, like the tremors of an earthquake, forcing the hot tears out of her body, but they didn't come from behind her eyes. They came from the depths of her insides, drained from her fingertips. She thought of the contractions that had brought T. J. to life, and how the doctor had said, "Push! Push!" It was worse when you couldn't locate the pain, the swelling and dying, swelling and dying; the pain was all-encompassing.

And when her body decided to be still—wore itself out, perhaps—the tears wouldn't stop pouring. Clay turned loose of her at last and found a box of tissues for them, drying them both off, their faces, necks, shoulders, and then wiping Leah's eyes again, because the tears kept coming. This did about as much good, Leah thought, as trying to dry yourself in a rain with a cotton swab.

"You'll feel better now," said Clay, sitting back on the floor beside her.

"No, I don't. I feel worse."

"I kept thinking you had to cry sometime."

"You didn't."

Clay didn't say anything for a moment. He bent his head, and finally, he seemed to speak to the floor. "I had to hold up. For you."

"No, you didn't," she cried. "Do you know how I felt, watching you jump right back into the mainstream when I could hardly drag myself out of bed? It was like—I don't know—like both of us were in body casts, but you got up and put your clothes on and went down the hall turning somersaults. It made me feel so—so *wronged*, somehow. Either you weren't hurt to start with, or there was something awful about me that kept me from moving on, too. It wasn't fair! God wasn't fair to punish me and not you!" She was sobbing, but her mind and body had fused again, and she had at least enough control to keep the electric current in her down to a mild trembling.

"Do you still not understand? God wasn't punishing either one of us, or T. J., either." Clay was facing her now. Leah could feel it, but her eyes were closed in tight, wet slits. "It just happened, that's all. Maybe it *wasn't* fair. But what about life *is* fair? What did we do to deserve being born in the first place? Or to have T. J. for six years? We were happy, Leah, then, and before then. I don't know that we deserved to be happy any more than we deserved to be sad when we lost T. J. I can't believe that his death came as punishment for something we'd done, any more than I can believe that his life was some sort of a reward to us."

"I prayed," Leah said. She choked on the words. "When he was hit, I prayed that he wouldn't die. It was the most earnest prayer I'd ever prayed. God could've made him live."

"Maybe," said Clay. "I don't know. Maybe God can make roses grow up through the snow, but I've never seen it. He lets the roses take their natural course. Every living thing dies. Why T. J. had to die so young, I don't know."

"Is that how you got by, just not asking?"

"Would it have been easier if we knew why?"

"I think so."

"I don't. It wouldn't bring T. J. back. Sure, I like for things to make sense, but T. J.'s gone, and we're left. That's the bottom line." He touched her chin, turning it up toward him, and said, "Let him go, Leah."

"No, I can't."

"Let him go."

She was not an earthquake now; she was a geyser, an endless source of hot tears.

"How did *you* do it? That's what I can't, for the life of me, understand!"

He looked away again, letting his hand drop. "You still don't believe that I was hurt, too."

"You got over it."

"You mean I went on living, or trying to, and I went on believing that God was good, instead of blaming him. I gave up trying to answer the unanswerable question. I accepted T. J.'s death as a fact of life. All right, I did all that. And still, losing him was darkest, cruelest, ugliest . . . " he took a long breath, and the rest came out just above a whisper: "I never told him good-bye."

The tears stopped. They stopped all at once—a faucet turned off—but the effect was a pitcher emptied to the last drop. Leah was spent. She wondered if she could ever cry again. "I wish you'd said that a year ago," she told him.

He took her hand between both of his. "You were so fragile, I thought you'd crack if I breathed. I'd just lost T. J. I couldn't lose you. If I was strong, it was for you." Then, as if he'd just thought of it, he said, "It was because of you, too. I'd lost T. J., but I still had you. That was enough to make me want to go on. More than enough." He pressed her hand to his lips. "But I never told you that, did I?"

Her throat was dry. She could still taste salt. "Let's go to the kitchen and get something to drink," she said.

Clay got up and flipped on the lights. The room turned yellow-gold, warm, safe, and Leah felt suddenly like a stranger in it, sitting cross-legged on the floor, in a sea of used tissues. She'd used most of a box, and the evidence had accumulated in scattered heaps, like the piles of paper flowers they used for decorating homecoming floats in high school.

Her knees felt watery when she stood. She took a couple of

wobbly steps, like a newborn calf. "Look." She pointed to the white tissue wads on the floor. "I cried out a whole year tonight. No wonder I'm drained. There it is, on the floor."

Clay got a wastebasket and scooped up handfuls of crumpled tissues, seeking out a single runaway, under the chair, under the dresser. He put his foot into the wastebasket and pressed all the air out, cutting the basketful by two thirds.

"Maybe there wasn't so much there, after all," said Leah.

"Anyway," Clay told her, "it's gone."

"Funeral homes all smell the same."

Leah tightened her fingers around Clay's arm as they entered through the heavy wooden doors, inlaid with stained glass. It seemed like the natural thing to do, to hold onto Clay for support. She remembered, out of the blur of events surrounding T. J.'s funeral, the way she had secured herself to his arm as if that were all that anchored her to the ground. Clay had been so quiet, with vacant eyes. But his arm had been her tie to reality.

"It's the smell of the flowers," said Clay.

"What?"

"The flowers. That's why funeral homes all smell the same."

"Yes. That's it."

As they reached the chamber where Ben's body lay in state, the air reeked with the fragrance of funeral flowers, like heavy perfume. "Did you ever see such a crowd, and so many flowers *already*?" Leah heard one woman say to another. Visitors had only been admitted an hour ago, but the room was packed.

It was the same with T. J., Leah thought. Walls of carnations and glads, mingled voices pitched just above a whisper. And the scented air, so sweet that it made you heady. She was beginning to wonder if it had been wise for her to come here, if she would be able to handle it, even now, and then she saw Catherine at the other end of the room. Mrs. Kent, the pastor's wife, was talking to her, and perhaps it was simply the contrast of Catherine next to the large-boned woman who was almost as tall as her husband, but Catherine looked so fragile that all at once Leah could think of nothing except to protect her.

"Over there," she said to Clay, and he maneuvered them through the crowd. Catherine saw them, and reached out for Leah with one hand, for Clay with the other, pulling them into a little circle that included Mrs. Kent. They said their hellos all around. Then the three who had come to comfort Catherine fell silent, and, true to character, Catherine took the lead.

"I don't know what I would've done without you two last night," she said, and then to Mrs. Kent, "or without Reverend Kent, either. They were all wonderful."

"I'm glad you had them with you," said the pastor's wife, who, Leah thought, appeared to be more comfortable with this than she and Clay. "And you know that you can call on Owen and me, any time at all."

Leah hadn't heard anyone speak of the pastor as Owen before, although she'd read and heard the name, Reverend Owen Kent, time after time. Of course his wife would call him Owen. What else would she call him? It just had an unfamiliar ring to it. People had a way of looking at ministers that wasn't fair, and Leah guessed she'd been one of the worst. Last night Reverend Kent had been just another friend of Ben Anderson's, like her and Clay. He had no immunity to the pain of losing a friend, and he had no answers to why this had happened. That was, perhaps, the biggest revelation of all to Leah, that the pastor didn't understand why any more than she did.

The *why* didn't seem so all-consuming today. Leah couldn't help thinking how frail Catherine looked, Catherine, who had always been a pillar, a support to whoever needed her. Now the pressing questions seemed to be, How will Catherine manage alone? What will this do to her? Can we help her? Maybe the question should never be, *Why?* Just, *What next?*

"Did you get any sleep?" she asked Catherine, for lack of anything else to say.

"Yes, a little. Well, not much. But I did take a nap after lunch."

"Did you get in touch with Ben's sister?"

"Yes, I stayed up till one-thirty to call her, and she called back this morning, after she'd considered coming for the funeral. It's too far and too expensive for just a few days. I discouraged it. She's going to come for a visit this summer. That'll be nice. She can stay a couple of weeks then. We haven't seen her in five years." She strained for a little laugh. "It's so hard to stop saying 'we.'"

"I wish you had some family nearby," said Leah.

"I have friends."

Leah remembered her family and Clay's family, their outpourings of grief. Their presence had provided a thin veneer of comfort, and she wished that for Catherine. But it was true that Catherine had been the real standby, Catherine, and of course, Clay.

Clay hadn't said much this evening, and now Leah noticed the strain on his face. He was not the kind who would fidget, but the restless tension was there, just the same.

"It's stuffy in here," said Leah.

It was a hint, and Clay took it. "Yes, very crowded. I think I'll step out in the hall for a minute. Catherine, do you need anything?"

"No, thanks."

Mrs. Kent excused herself, as well. "If I can locate Owen, we have to make a stop at the hospital before church tonight. Mr. Wen, one of our internationals, had an emergency appendectomy this afternoon, and we need to check on him."

She and Catherine exchanged a few words about the funeral tomorrow, and as she left, she said, "It was nice to see you, Leah. We've missed you."

"Thank you." Leah believed that she meant it.

Others came by to offer kind words to Catherine, and Leah stayed at her side. "Let's sit down," Catherine said, after a few minutes, and they found two chairs. More visitors, more condolences. Then, abruptly, Catherine said, "I've got to find a rest room," and she hurried out of the room.

When she returned, she looked weak and washed out. "Are you all right?" Leah asked.

"I was sick, but I'm all right now."

"Sit down," said Leah. "This is all just too much."

"No, no, that's not it." Catherine laid her hand on Leah's arm. "Leah, God is good to us. I wish you could believe it. He never leaves us hopeless."

Leah nodded, trying to understand what kind of hope Catherine could find, just one day after her husband's death.

"I'll miss Ben. I'll miss him so much. But, Leah, I'm carrying his child."

As they left the funeral home, stepping out into the sweet darkness, heavy with spring, Leah told Clay that Catherine was pregnant.

"A miracle," Clay said. The tight muscles of his face relaxed a little. "I wonder if Ben knew."

"Catherine said he did." She wondered if Clay was thinking what had been her first thought, that the irony was too great, that death was cruel and unjust to cheat a man out of ever seeing his child.

But the corners of Clay's mouth worked into a smile, and he nodded. "I'm glad he knew. That's wonderful."

Some people said a cup was half empty, Leah thought; others, like Clay and Catherine, always said it was half full. The simple truth was, both *were* right. You just chose your point of view. And, yes, you had a choice.

Catherine had lost her husband, but she would have the child she'd wanted so much. In that sense, Ben would live. Leah slipped her hand into Clay's. She had lost her child, but she had a husband who had loved her through the coldest, bitterest season of their lives, and she knew now that she hadn't stopped loving him, either. She wondered why she hadn't seen it before.

18

George didn't come to class for several days. After he missed his second test, Clay got his phone number from admissions. That night he called his house.

"Yes, George is here," his mother said, when Clay told her who he was, "but I don't know that he'll come to the phone." Hers was a shrill, anxious voice. "I think he's quit school."

"I'd like to talk to him anyway," said Clay.

"Well, I'll ask him."

Clay held the phone for what seemed like five minutes and listened to the blare of a television sit-com in the background. Finally, George came on the line with a sluggish hello.

"Hello, George. This is Clay Padgett. I've been worried about you."

"Why are you calling me, Dr. Padgett?" He sounded annoyed.

"I told you, I was worried. Hey, doctors on television travel five hundred miles to convince a patient that he needs treatment. So why can't I call a sharp student who's going to flunk my class if he doesn't get back?"

"Yeah," George said, absently.

"I see you're in no mood to kid around."

He didn't respond to that. He said, "I thought my mother told you. I've quit."

"Why are you giving up, George?"

George's voice registered a little more spirit. "As if you didn't know."

"I know Ben's death has hit you hard. It's been a blow to a lot of people, including me. I know a little about what you're going through."

"No, you don't. You don't know the whole story. Or maybe you do. Probably everybody knows by now. Anyway, I can't come back to school."

He sounded shaky, and Clay wished they were face to face. Maybe he could help George brace up and work through what was eating at him. But the telephone was the only connection he had now, and even at that, he was about to lose George on the other end.

"Sounds as if you're not just giving up on school. I think you're giving up on yourself."

George was silent.

"Come on back to school," said Clay.

"I'm already too far behind," George finally said.

Clay took a deep, exasperated breath. "You never give your instructors any credit. I'd be willing to let any student make up his work if he came to me with a good reason and a good attitude. Within a reasonable length of time, of course. I know you've missed several classes, but you haven't lost the quarter yet. Not if you get back tomorrow. Your teachers aren't cold stone, George. Give us a chance."

He made a sarcastic laugh. "You know, Ben said just about the same thing to me. Right before he died. I let him down, and I'll let you down, too."

"You'll be letting me down if I don't see you in class tomorrow."

"I don't know," said George.

"I'll keep the half hour before class time free," Clay told him, "just in case you get there early."

George did come early, carrying his books in the crook of his arm. "I thought I'd find out how much I'd missed," he said. "I've checked with a couple of other teachers. Turns out I'm not too far behind."

"You can catch up in here, too," Clay told him.

They spent a few minutes going over what the class had covered in George's absence. "On Monday, I'd like to give you both of the make-up tests, if that's enough time," Clay said when they'd finished.

George nodded, as if to say, *A piece of cake.* Then he slapped shut his book and slumped over with his elbows on his knees. "Wish it all made as much sense as trig," he said, talking down to the floor.

Clay wondered if people like him and George, whose minds were geared toward the exactness that math and science provided, just naturally had a hard time with the aspects of life— and death—that wouldn't fit into a box with a label. He wondered if statistics would bear that out. Or perhaps it was that no one really knew how to handle the situations that defied reason, but the logical minds worried more, felt a sense of failure because they *didn't* understand.

"You're pretty shaken now," said Clay, "but that's not a permanent condition. Ben's death may not ever make sense to you, but it'll get easier to accept. I know that to be a fact."

"I don't *want* to accept it." George looked up with cold granite eyes. "I can't ever let myself forget that I'm responsible for Ben's death."

Clay said, "That's too heavy to hang on yourself."

"It's the truth. If I hadn't run off like a madman, Ben wouldn't have had that heart attack."

Clay rubbed the bones around his eyes and prayed for the right words. He'd been so sure he could appeal to George's reason if only George would give him the chance, but now they were face to face, and he'd never felt so inadequate for a task.

"I wish I could say that you didn't have any part in it," he said. "I tend to think that Ben would've had this heart attack, anyway, but not even the doctors could tell you for sure. The point is, flogging yourself for his death isn't going to bring Ben back. It's just going to mess up your chance to benefit from his life. Ben had a kind of investment in you, you know."

George hardly seemed to be listening. He said, "I made a terrible, stupid mistake."

Something tugged at Clay then, reaching into a deep, hidden chamber for words he had not said before or perhaps even thought. "You can make mistakes, George. You can even be weak. You're getting this from a good source. I never thought I was allowed. When my son died, I told myself I had to be strong for my wife. So I was a pillar of strength. Was I ever. The trouble was, no one, not even my wife, knew I was hurting. Don't cut yourself off like that. People want to help. People forgive. God forgives. All of us are weak at times, but that doesn't mean that we don't have potential, as long as we don't give up." He took a long breath, but he couldn't stop without saying one more thing. "Suppose I'd been in Ben's place, and you and Ben were having this conversation. What would he say to you?"

George thought about it. "He'd probably tell me not to get bogged down in all of this. He had a way of shrugging things off. Not that he didn't care. You just couldn't call him a worrier."

"What else would he say?"

George's lips parted into the start of a grin. "He'd probably say, 'See you in church Sunday.' "

"Yeah," said Clay.

George got up, shifting, wobbling a little like a marionette, Clay thought. "We're gonna be late to class," George said. "I'll try, but it's all such a hassle. I hate hassles."

"Don't we all."

That afternoon Shirley Nettleton plopped a thick bound booklet on Clay's desk and said, "This is it, and only two weeks late, which is better than average for university printing."

Clay picked up the report and thumbed through it. "Looks impressive. I wonder if it says anything."

"You know it does. We did a good job, Clay. We can all be proud, and you, most of all."

Clay ran his finger down the table of contents. The committee had been thorough, yes. If he had it to do again, he wouldn't know how to proceed any differently. They had made some bold recommendations, some excellent ones. If the administration acted on any of their suggestions, he'd consider it worth their efforts, but particularly if the changes were made concerning scholarship students. Maybe a future George Kirby would find the first year a little easier than George had.

"Sit down, Shirley. I forgot my manners." Clay smiled. He never had been able to think of Shirley as just a fellow teacher. As hard-nosed as she was, there was, nonetheless, a strong reminder of a lady from the Old South.

"I don't have time, and don't you get up, either," she said as he started to rise from his chair. "I just wanted to deliver our report, fresh off the press, and find out what you thought about it."

"It's fine, Shirley." He sank back. "But I have to wonder, will anyone read it?"

"I think so," she frowned, considering. "Yes, I do. This is a good school, Clay. More responsive than most, to students and staff alike." She flattened her palms on his desk, leaning forward, and her voice turned velvet with persuasion. "No university's perfect, and I've been connected with enough of them to know, but Jackson State is a wonderful place to settle and grow in your profession, if you're not too impatient."

She straightened up, still touching the desk with her fingertips. "Forgive me, Clay. I'm not lecturing you. I just made this speech to someone else. You remember Carmen Kennedy, the pretty redhead in dramatic arts? Her mother and I were friends, and I've tried to be a friend to Carmen. She's a talented girl, but one of these who's always looking for greener pastures. You know the type? Carmen's resigned her position here. Says she's moving back to Los Angeles. 'And what is wrong with Jackson State?' I asked her. Silly girl. She said, 'It's no fun.'"

Reverend Kent was trying to outline his Sunday sermon, but

he kept darting off task. He made a call to one of his members who was recovering from surgery at home, a call that could've waited till tonight. Then one of his deacons phoned about repaving the parking lot, and they talked for a long time about nothing that really mattered. Later, after the church secretary had gone and he should've left, too, he got out and walked around the building, pulling weeds. Then he went back to his office and jotted down a note for the secretary: "Call yardman."

When Clay Padgett knocked on the office door, Reverend Kent was delighted.

"I was on my way home, and I just took a chance that you'd be in," said Clay. "What are you doing here so late?"

He laughed. "Maybe I had a vision that you were going to drop by."

Clay sank back in the big upholstered chair where people sat when they bared their souls and cried their bitterest tears. But it wasn't going to be that kind of encounter with Clay, Reverend Kent could tell. Clay's manner was easy, and his smile was not the forced one that Reverend Kent had noticed so often. They talked about the church's paving project and about the end of school. Was Clay going to teach the summer session? Reverend Kent asked him. No, maybe he and Leah could take a long trip if he didn't have that commitment.

"I guess you'll be needing a replacement in the college and career department," Clay said, all at once.

Reverend Kent's face became one wide smile. "Now I know why you're here."

"I always said you were very perceptive."

"And I always said you had good instincts."

Clay knew that Catherine wouldn't be able to work with the group by herself. He also knew that he had been away too long. He had waited for Leah, but maybe Leah needed to see him make the first move toward normalcy, if there were such a thing.

"I can't think of anyone in the church who could relate to that group the way you can," Reverend Kent told him.

"Ben was such a natural for the job," said Clay, "but he's gone, and someone needs to do it. I don't want the work he started to fall apart."

They were interrupted by the phone then, but Clay said, "I'm leaving, anyway."

"Just a minute." Reverend Kent said hello, and then, "Hello! Listen, would you mind holding for one moment?" He put his hand over the mouthpiece and told Clay, "This is a call I need to take."

"Sure. I'm finished, anyway. See you later."

"See you, and listen, thanks."

"Hello! Someone was just leaving. Thanks for holding on."

"That's all right. I hope I'm not bothering you, but do you have a minute?" Leah's voice was a little uncertain but not unhappy.

"Of course I do. If I didn't have a minute, I'd take one anyway. I'm glad to hear from you."

"I've put you off so many times. I wanted to apologize." She started out as if she'd rehearsed, but then she made a little laugh, and Reverend Kent knew she was finding her lines along the way. "It's been such a complicated year, and I haven't handled it well at all, but I'm doing better. Yesterday I went into T. J.'s room for the first time. It was hard, but at least I did it."

"Sounds like a good sign."

She said, "You told me once that I could be a big help to Catherine. Well, as usual, she's the one who's helping me."

"I'm sure it works both ways. Don't sell yourself short, Leah. Catherine *needs* that. That's how *she* thrives."

"I guess."

He asked her about school. It was frustrating, she told him, winding up the year, knowing she hadn't put enough into it. But she was looking for a restful summer, and next year would be better.

"I won't keep you any longer," she said. "I just wanted to thank you for not giving up on me."

236

"Call me any time," he told her. "I'll never give up on you."

He straightened up his desk, thinking how strange it was, the way God worked in people and through people. It was what he believed, the message he preached, and yet sometimes it took a thunderbolt to make him see the truth in it. He glanced at his outline before tucking it in the bottom drawer. Tomorrow, he could start with plenty of motivation. He might even have a new sermon.

19

This close to the end of school, the crisp, glassy mornings couldn't last, but, so far, the children were still wearing jackets. Except for a few, like Edward, and like Wendell, who was Edward's shadow anytime they were out of the classroom.

The two boys were passing a football when Leah drove into the parking lot, but Edward tucked the ball under his arm when Wendell rushed to meet her. This time Edward was the shadow, sauntering over like a tired old man.

"Can I help you carry something?" Wendell wanted to know. His voice was bright, full of the hope and trust that children wear so well.

"I don't need any help this morning," she said. Wendell exaggerated a pout. "But if you happen to be around this afternoon, I'll have a big stack of science notebooks to take home." She turned to Edward. "Have you finished yours?"

Edward nodded. Leah could see a grin trying to take form, but Edward wouldn't let it. He wasn't supposed to be proud of himself, of course, not proud of doing his homework, anyway.

"I helped him!" Wendell put in.

"*Daddy* helped me," Edward corrected him, "but mostly I did it by myself."

"Tie my shoe," Wendell said to his brother, and Edward stooped down, muttering that he'd be glad when Wendell learned how to tie.

Leah looked at the dirty laces and the shoe itself, worn out at the toe. Edward's were the same. When other children were bouncing in their new tennis shoes bought for summer, Edward and Wendell were just about down to bare skin. There ought to be some kind of school fund for situations like this. She'd ask Mr. Carlton about it today, even if she was a whole school year late in doing so.

She noticed their jeans, too, with holes at the knees. Edward's knit shirt seemed to be in good shape, but Wendell's was so faded that you couldn't make out what the printing on it was supposed to be. Both shirts could use a good washing. And neither of the boys had jackets, she suspected.

"Aren't you chilly?" she asked them. Her own blazer felt just right.

"Naw, we've been running," said Edward.

"Edward has a new jacket, anyway, if he'd wanted to wear it," said Wendell.

"Really? How about you?"

"I've got *his.*"

Leah smiled. It was a good thing that Wendell didn't mind the hand-me-downs that were, more often than not, dirty, torn, ill-fitting, and out of style, because that was all he had. Wendell was cute, as it was, but Leah thought how she'd like to see him, for once, dressed a little more appropriately. He'd have a much better chance of getting off to a good start in kindergarten if he had some decent clothes. It occurred to her that *that* was something she could fix.

"Wendell," she said, "there are a lot of clothes at my house for a little boy just your size. You'd be doing me a favor if you'd take them. Could I bring them to you tomorrow?"

"Sure!"

She asked Edward, "You don't think your father would mind, do you?"

"He won't mind. He'd be glad. Wendell never gets any new clothes." Edward showed more interest in this than she'd seen in him at all.

"The clothes I have aren't new, but they're in good shape,"

Leah said. "They're mostly play clothes, jeans and shirts and football jerseys. And there's a jacket in the bunch. One of those nylon windbreakers with an Atlanta Falcons symbol on it. It's red."

"Tomorrow?" Wendell asked, grinning.

"Yes. Be here when I get to school, and I'll give them to you."

"I'll bring you some roses, too."

"Roses? Where will you get them?" she wanted to know.

"They're growing in Miz Dortch's yard. She won't care."

"I thought it was too early for roses."

"I don't know," Wendell chirped. "Miz Dortch has a rosebush. I'll show you. I'll bring you a *bow*-kay. But you've gotta be careful, cause they have stickers."

Her classroom was stuffy, and she got the windows up, first thing. The air felt new in her face, clean in her lungs. *Roses.* It couldn't be that late in the year. But it was. It was nearly the end of school, and like every other year's end, Leah was a little reluctant to see her motley crew disband. Maybe that was another good sign.

Roses. Roses in the snow. Where had she heard that? She couldn't remember. Maybe it was a line from a poem. But it didn't matter. Roses didn't grow in the snow, of course. They lent their beauty for a short season, and then they were gone. But the system never failed. Spring always found tow-headed boys with pricked fingers holding up the new blooms to ladies who smiled at them. It was like a promise. It was something you could count on.